Pit Stops

Crossing the Country with Loren the Rescue Bully

Michelle Sathe

Pit Stops: Crossing the Country with Loren the Rescue Bully

First Edition

Cover design: Lynn Ammerman

Front cover - main photo: Will Davison

Front and back covers - inset photos: Michelle Sathe

Interior design: Michelle Sathe

All interior photos by Michelle Sathe (except for Murphy and Daisy's photo, courtesy of Hello Bully)

ISBN 978-0-615-38699-7

Printed in the United States of America

To Wayde Dyer, for loving this crazy dog lady and taking care of our pack

To Nancy Anderson of The Brittany Foundation, for rescuing Loren and thousands of dogs like her

To Yvonne Allbee, for being my biggest cheerleader and starting me on this path

To my Brittany Foundation family - April Lund, Heather Mohr, Leeanne Shinn, Rene Ruston, Gina Tucci, Karen Kennedy, et al. - for loving homeless dogs as if they were your own

To my sober mountain sisters - Gail K., Liz B., Ronni W. and Eileen B. - for encouraging me to trudge this road of happy destiny

To Jim and Rose Sathe, for AAA, Gidget and indulging my adventurous spirit

To Margo's Bark Root Beer, Dog-o-Scopes, and all my friends and family who made this dream a reality

To all the rescuers, shelter staff, advocates and volunteers we met along the way, for sharing your stories and your spirit

To the millions of animals who die in shelters or suffer at the hands of cruel humans, for letting me be your voice. RIP.

To Stefan Niemczyk, for giving Loren what I never could

To Loren, for being the best four-legged friend anyone could ask for - may your road ahead always be happy, sweet girl

Foreword

When asked to write the foreword for this story of Michelle's journey with her companion, Loren, I was to keep two things in mind. One, to discuss briefly how the pit bull went from one of America's favorite dogs to the most feared, victimized, and destroyed in our public shelter system. The other was to relate how the efforts of just one individual or the rescuing of one individual dog can be so crucial to raising the value of these animals in our human society.

What is a pit bull anyway? I think that the most accurate definition is one I heard from Don Cleary of the National Canine Research Council, that a pit bull is a folk devil. A character set in a larger tale that has been taking place in America since at least since the late 1800s.

A social construct has been built, that of a dangerous, vicious killer of a dog. All positive canine traits have been stripped away - loyalty, devotion, friendship, obedience, trustworthiness - while only negative traits remained.

The pit bull has ultimately become something of a mythological villain, both beloved and victimized by the human race.

Human beings need villains. I guess it helps us feel successful in our quest for goodness, or godliness. The quest for morality is naturally human. I suspect that this stems from the need to understand. Creating villains, though, seems to undermine the idea of personal responsibility.

After all, if the boogie man is real, there is really nothing you can do about it. It's not "your" fault. If the dogs are at fault for their behavior solely because of their genetics ("they are born with it", or "it's in their blood"), then why do we need to learn how to care for them properly? Why should they even be allowed to live? Pit bulls have paid a very high price for this philosophy.

More practically, a pit bull is the term used to define a group of dogs that meet subjective, visual characteristics. This is a term that has also taken on the image and character of the substandard owner and those that are associated with the seedy world of crime, cruelty and senselessness. Not entirely, but certainly most loudly.

The media, since the July 1987 issue of *Sports Illustrated* magazine, has shouted this image through its 24/7 information megaphone. That issue had, as its cover, the face of a brindle dog with a focus on its shiny white teeth, warning the photographer of the urgency to snap that shot.

By the end of that year, every major media news publication wrote damning stories of dogs labeled as 'pit bulls.'

It seemed that regardless of the breed of dog, if the behavior was inappropriate, or dangerous, that dog was a pit bull. If a dog was a hero, friend or companion…well, it was the quintessential family dog, not a pit bull. Good dog traits like loyalty, trust and friendliness were taken away from these short-haired muscular mutts and their papered canine brethren: the American Pit Bull Terrier, American Staffordshire Terrier, Staffordshire Bull Terrier, et al.

It may sound strange, but as it turns out, Michael Vick, the professional football player that served time for operating a kennel to supply dogs for fighting, seemed to play the catalyst for the animal welfare movement and dog-loving Americans across the country to change the course of a national debate.

Vick's arrest and conviction put the plight of these dogs on the kitchen table of mainstream America. People from all walks of life were shocked and horrified by the detailed and gruesome accounts of Vick's sordid choice of entertainment. Pit bulls finally started receiving some good press. Even *Sports Illustrated* changed its tune. In December 2008, the magazine ran a wonderful story by Jim Gorant about the recovery of some survivors of Bad Newz Kennels. On the cover was a photo of a sweet pit bull named Jasmine.

For the first time dogs recovered from this type of crime were going to get a chance at being evaluated as individual, sentient beings. And since then, there has been a national trend from municipal shelters, animal control agencies, law enforcement, and local to federal politics, to see that the dogs are treated as victims of cruelty and not willing participants or villains.

I feel lucky to have played a small role in this national debate. It has led me to meet some wonderful people filled with compassion and a drive to lead an effort to help us all become more responsible with the animals that depend on us. Michelle is one of these people, and her story of traveling the country to learn about pit bull issues, and promote a wonderful dog named Loren in a quest to find her a permanent and loving family to call home, is a touching one.

You don't have to love dogs or own dogs in order to help our country achieve a time of no more homeless pets. All you need to do is to be responsible in digesting and disseminating information.

If I have learned one thing by working on the Best Friends campaign Pit Bulls: Saving America's Dog under the wing of a pioneer in animal law, Ledy VanKavage, it is that one person CAN make a difference, whether it's being a voice for animals or voting.

As Ledy will proudly broadcast – 'politics is not a spectator sport!'

If you are a dog person, you will be tickled by Michelle's accounting of all of the people she meets along the way due to the captivating nature of a homeless canine named Loren.

"I marveled at Loren's ability to make us friends. No one ever just came up to me and started talking. What a blessing she was. How impossibly lonely I'd be without her."

Read this book. Cry if you have to, but finish it. Then go to your local shelter or rescue and help your community.

You will be well rewarded!

Sincerely,

Ed Fritz
Campaign Specialist, Pit Bulls: Saving America's Dog
Best Friends Animal Society

Table of Contents

Introduction: An Unexpected Love

Turning 40 can make people do wild things. Buy a Harley. Switch careers. Turn in their mate for a younger model. I didn't want to do anything so cliché or potentially damaging.

No, when I hit that milestone on May 10, 2009, I wanted to take the great American road trip I'd promised myself I would always do, but never quite found time for before. Just me and the open road. Seeing the things I'd always dreamt about, such as The Grand Canyon and Niagara Falls, and eating authentic regional foods like gumbo in New Orleans and BBQ in the south.

Since I had no kids, a busy boyfriend, and only a part-time newspaper job, courtesy of the recession, I figured it was the perfect time to make my getaway.

I love traveling solo. Actually, that's not entirely true. I love traveling with dogs. Quiet, sweet, up-for-anything companions that don't laugh at you for playing air guitar. Sidekicks that don't constantly ask how long it is until we get there or complain about a hotel's less than perfect sheets.

My first dog, a black lab named Jake, was an ideal co-pilot during our many road trips in Southern California, as well as to Colorado and Idaho to vacation with my parents. Since Jake had passed on, this time I would take Buster, my four-year old Staffordshire Terrier mix, and write a book about our journey, killing two things on the bucket list with one stone.

Or so I thought…

***

In January 2008, I was a freelance producer for SCVTV in Valencia, California, and tried to air stories on animal issues whenever possible. I had heard of The Brittany Foundation, a no-kill dog rescue, for many years, but I had never been to their Agua Dulce sanctuary.

The morning was cold by Southern California standards, rain that turned into a light snow. Nancy Anderson, Brittany Foundation's founder and operator, was in a bit of a frenzied state. Donning a heavy jacket over her petite yet stocky frame and a beanie over her shoulder-length blonde locks, Nancy ran about the small two-bedroom home that served as rescue's headquarters, conferring with volunteers Heather Mohr and Rene Succa-Ruston about whether the weather would make for a less than ideal segment.

"I don't want us to look bad," Nancy said nervously. "Maybe it's too cold. Maybe it's too grey."

About 20 little senior dogs scuttled around her feet on the painted concrete floor. Some were missing eyes, some had cataracts so advanced they glowed. There was a tiny brown Chihuahua with paralyzed legs dragging behind her and a toothless Yorkie whose tongue hung out the right side of his mouth. More dogs congregated together on the many beds spread out on the floor or on couches draped with fuzzy blankets, some napping, some looking on wide-eyed, crazy canine claymation characters brought to life.

Alex, the cameraman, and I assured Nancy the weather was not a problem for us. Professionally, I didn't want the hassle of rescheduling, but personally, I understood where she was coming from.

"It's up to you," I told her, praying silently we could move forward.

Nancy decided to let us shoot and gave us a tour of the facility. The Brittany Foundation, located on three acres in the Southern California desert, had a rustic ranch feel, with scrubby rolling hills behind the main house and rocky, red dirt roads leading to and from the rescue. The compound's ground was blanketed with three inches of pea gravel and boasted many trees, which were bare this winter.

She toured us around the back kennels first, where dozens of small dogs scrambled for attention. Every one had a little sweater to ward off the chill and their large kennels were scrupulously clean. The front was the same, except the kennels were slightly larger, 12' x 12', and most housed single big dogs: a greying black lab mix named Buffy, a massive Jack Russell look-alike named Charlie, and several pit bulls or pit mixes.

The kennels were lined in plywood around the bottom half, while the top half was an open-air pattern of two inch mesh squares. Inside, the perimeter was lined in brick-colored concrete steps and the center filled with pea gravel to draw away moisture. Like the small dogs, each big dog's kennel had its own Igloo dog house with fresh bedding, blankets spread on the steps for al fresco napping, balls, rope toys, Nylabones, and a stainless steel water bucket. It was a pretty nice set up.

There were a few pairs occupying the kennels, such as Dana and Hannah, a pit bull and her hyena-like mixed breed daughter from the streets of South Central Los Angeles. Tommy, a lab/pit mix, and Skylar, his handicapped pitty girlfriend born missing part of her front right paw, were a particularly cute couple. Mostly, though, the big dogs lived alone, like Doza, a buff red and white pit bull with cropped ears, eyes like actor Terrence Howard and a body like The Rock, looking dapper in his blue and yellow striped rugby shirt.

Then there was Loren. Sprung from her kennel, donning a knitted pink sweater, she immediately hugged my legs and started kissing my face. Though only a year and a half old, Loren had wise amber eyes that seemed to peer into my soul. The red and white pit bull was strong, yes, but sweet and somehow delicate, too, with her lanky, slightly awkward body, freckly pink nose, and floppy little ears.

"We picked up Loren from the Lancaster shelter," Nancy explained. "She was a stray. She loves people."

I could tell. I reluctantly pried Loren off me with a final kiss, then kept moving along the kennels to finish the taping.

Ultimately, the segment aired without a hitch. I, however, was never the same.

***

I emailed Nancy about volunteering within days of filming. Already a board member for Bow-Wows & Meows, a non-profit organization that hosts an annual pet fair in Santa Clarita where we adopt out L.A. County Shelter animals, I longed to do something more hands-on with homeless dogs. Not at a shelter where they euthanized animals, though. That would be too sad for me. The Brittany Foundation was just what I had been looking for.

Within weeks, I was cleaning out kennels and helping out at the ranch, driving an hour and a half each way from my home in Pine Mountain Club. I loved interacting with the big dogs, going for walks and playing ball. For being cooped up in a kennel most of their lives, they were all surprisingly well-behaved and, not surprisingly, extremely grateful for the attention.

Each was endearing in his or her own way. Kirby, the fuzzy black terrier who didn't like most men but loved the ladies, would do a little twirl when he saw me coming. Doza could catch a Frisbee with the grace and speed of a champion, while Buffy could melt stone with her soulful black eyes and effective begging tricks.

Loren won me over with sheer affection and her cute pink nose, sprinkled with dusty rose freckles. I'd take her out of the kennel and into the large run area, a 2100' square foot rectangle with rocks to climb and bushes to sniff, which we dubbed "Project Dogway" (so the dogs could strut their stuff for potential adopters). She'd immediately hug me, standing on her tip toes to smother my face with kisses, then collapse halfway onto my lap, a big, wide goofy grin spread across her face. She didn't really care much about playing. I'd throw a ball or toss a Frisbee and Loren would stare at it blankly, barely moving her head to see where it landed, much less chase after it.

She wasn't really into walking, either. Unlike her canine counterparts, who couldn't wait to get out and sniff along the dirt trails for 15-20 minutes, Loren would excitedly pull on her leash to get out of the main kennel door, but once you started heading off the compound, would drag her feet on the pea gravel before she laid down completely in protest, crossing her front paws. After that, it was a stop and start routine, with Loren stalling and having to be coaxed to move another ten feet. Once we got past the driveway, which had eight-foot-high stucco fencing, she was usually good to go, trotting along the trail happily in her gangly way, but getting Loren there was quite a battle.

Loren always wanted to cuddle, which we would do in her kennel, in Project Dogway, wherever we could. I'd bring her an extra piece of chicken from Subway, since she was a little on the skinny side, and feed it to her in private so the others wouldn't see. It felt a bit illicit. I loved them all, but Loren was my favorite.

I longed to adopt her, but couldn't. My Buster and his older "brother" Sam, a male American Bulldog mix, didn't take too kindly to other dogs and truth be told, Loren didn't either. I may be a crazy dog lady, but I'm no Dog Whisperer - there's no way I could handle a three-way fight with that pack. It was hard enough when Buster and Sam got into their annual alpha scuffle, which usually resulted in torn flesh and expensive vet bills.

My heart ached for all the big Brittany dogs, that they weren't in homes and their chances of adoption seemed slim compared to the little dogs, who were regularly placed with families. Many of the big dogs had been there for years; Buffy, Tommy and Skylar almost their whole lives.

When it was cold, I worried about them. When it was hot, I worried about them. Were they suffering? Were they lonely? Did they get any love that day? For the first nine months of volunteering, I regularly cried about their predicament and lamented on canine karma - why did some dogs get the best homes while some dogs languished in rescues or worse, got killed in shelters? Why did some dogs get picked at adoption events when others would get overlooked or, like Loren, receive heavy interest but no follow-through?

I worried about Nancy, too. The recession was in full swing and she was taking in approximately half of the donations she usually received. She was down to a part-time kennel worker and us volunteers, who were sporadic at best. The work was hard enough, but Nancy was nearing 60 and it was especially tough on her, though she never talked about it, her stoic Minnesota upbringing prohibiting her from ever whining, at least to me.

Nancy crowned me the volunteer coordinator and slowly, after joining VolunteerMatch.org, an online service that offered free volunteer recruitment, as well as listing our needs in local publications, our volunteer base began to build. It wasn't every day, but most days of the week, the dogs had a volunteer to give them playtime, affection, and exercise, while Nancy had help.

My skin began to toughen, too. At the end of the day, when I'd volunteer, I'd hand out treats and tell them all I loved them, that they were good dogs. I'd look down the rows of kennels to see contented dogs resting and realized, for that day at least, all was okay in their world. They were secure, they were safe, they were walked or played with, they were fed and taken to the vet, they were loved by Nancy and the volunteers. Was it as good as being in a loving home of their own? No. But it was enough.

***

As my 40th birthday road trip plan began to take seed the fall of 2008, it hit me. I looked around at The Brittany Foundation dogs in their kennels, who were so excited when people came, to go for a 20 minute walk or a stretch of playtime in Dogway. They needed a vacation more than my dogs, who went for a thirty minute walk in the woods every day and had a huge yard to play in, when they weren't napping on the couch (Buster) or my king-size bed (Sam).

Yes, I would take a Brittany dog instead. But who? I looked around and knew instantly.

There was practically a halo over her kennel. Loren. The snuggle-poo. She would be perfect for getting through the long miles and cuddling up on lonely nights.

Over the next few months, the plan grew. I shared it with family and friends, more excited with each passing week. Not only would Loren and I travel for fun, we could spread a message about adopting homeless pets, especially pit bulls, which I knew were crowding the country's shelters and being killed in record numbers. Loren was such a sweetie, I was sure that just by interacting with her, people's perceptions about pit bulls could be changed for the positive.

I let the Brittany Foundation volunteers in on my idea to get their feedback before approaching Nancy, who I wasn't sure would be too keen on letting Loren go for that long. Though she had 90 dogs, she was fiercely protective of all of them. The plan was met with resounding acceptance, excitement, and encouragement.

When I presented the idea to Nancy during a volunteer dinner in October, to my surprise, she smiled and agreed immediately. Michele Buttelman, my boss at *The Signal*, not only said yes to my taking seven weeks off, she wanted to run weekly accounts of our adventures in the Sunday features page. Most importantly, my boyfriend Wayde was willing to take care of Sam and Buster in my absence.

My creative mind was spinning. I could get sponsors, I could start a website and a blog, and print postcards on how to help homeless pets that we would pass out on the road. It would be a movement. With all the publicity, Loren might even find a home by the time we were done.

There was a bounce in my step the next time I made my way through the big dog kennels at The Brittany Foundation.

"Loren," I sing-songed through the wire mesh doors of her kennels as I entered. "Guess what? We're taking a trip. Just you and me."

Her curious amber eyes looked deeply into mine as I kissed her fuzzy, freckled snout.

The same scene would play out every Saturday as I counted down the time: six months, three months, one month, then just six days until our departure date of May 15, 2009.

"I'm going to make you the most famous pit bull in America," I told her, "for all the right reasons."

The Grand Canyon & a Grand Failure

"Pawsome! Totally pawsome!"

It was so beautiful it brought tears to my eye. Layers of red, orange, bronze, green and gold rock, carved out in huge, flat-topped mountains and spread into crevices so deep, I could barely comprehend their recesses. A place of immense spirituality and incredible grace. The Grand Canyon.

I looked over at Stefanie Bjerregaard, a Brittany Foundation volunteer whom I'd met and hit it off with just before she moved to Salt Lake City in 2008. When I found out we share the same birthday, I invited her to meet us at the Grand Canyon to celebrate.

She brought along her boyfriend, Dave, and the four of stood at the south rim on Saturday, May 16, in silence.

Dave's hand affectionately patted Loren's head as we marveled at the awe-inspiring sight. I don't know if she was hot, happy or both, but Loren had a big grin on her face, too.

It had been almost 24 hours since we had left The Brittany Foundation. Loren was sprung from her kennel with much fanfare, as our sponsors Tim, Jessica and Oscar Youd of Margo's Bark Root Beer had met us to drop off a car magnet and introduce themselves. One hundred percent of their root beer profits benefit shelter dogs, so we were thrilled to have them on board, along with our second sponsor Dog-O-Scopes, a zodiac-themed dog tag company that also supports rescue.

Rene and Amber, another long-time Brittany Foundation volunteer, were also there to capture the moment on video, while Nancy ran around like a nervous mother sending her child off to camp for the first time. We packed the back of my black Toyota Tacoma, which had a shell, full of dog food, a crate, a dog bed, and toys for Loren along with two months worth of clothing and sundries for me.

The truck was quite a sight, festooned with hundreds of black and white paw print magnets family, friends and supporters had signed and purchased for $1 each. Between the magnets, sponsorships, my 40th birthday party, a garage sale and raffle hosted by my friends, and online donations from our website, we had raised close to $5,000 for the trip.

Loren bounded from her kennel, the rest of the big dogs barking like mad as she made her exit. She jumped into my car as if it were the most natural thing in the world, sniffing around, tail thumping, until she twirled around and settled in the front seat. I snapped on her donated Hip Hound Couture "Born to Bark" collar with a Ruffscue the Rescue Dog-O-Scopes tag engraved with my cell number and Nancy's landline. We were ready to go.

I hugged everyone goodbye. "Be safe," Nancy told me.

"Have fun, LoLo," Nancy said to Loren as she gave her farewell kisses through the window.

I smiled to myself. I had never heard Nancy call Loren or any of the big dogs a pet name before, just the little old house dogs. Beneath her crusty, tough as nails exterior, she really was a marshmallow.

We set out from the bumpy dirt roads of Agua Dulce for a 500-mile stretch of paved desert highways. For the first hour, Loren was my co-pilot, sitting in the front, alternately snoozing and getting up to check out the scenery rolling past us. Then she discovered the back cab, to which I had added a fluffy layer of pillow and blankets, and that was that. She disappeared to nap, only to come out for potty breaks along the way.

One such stop was Goffs, home of a very surreal, old-school gas station with a tropical motif, bright neon signage, and not much else. Their convenience market was overrun with German bikers in jeans and leather chaps. I was charged $6.50 for a bottle of iced tea, a banana, and a small bag of Cheetos.

"Extortionists, Loren, that's what they are," I said as I started the truck, popping open the tea and tearing into the Cheetos. I held a puff out to her and she sniffed it delicately before taking it ever so gently from my hand and crunching down on the new treat. I shared more than a few Cheetos with her and, less than an hour later, paid the price. My sweet Loren had gas that rivaled any full grown man.

"Oh my God, Loren," I said rolling down the window and nearly choking from a blast of hot desert air. I left it open for 20 seconds to dilute the offending odor before succumbing to the need for air conditioning. "Wow."

She looked at me, nonplussed, from her perch in the back seat, eyes slowly lowering into sleep.

The afternoon turned into evening as the endless miles of black asphalt surrounded by dry, beige dessert rolled along. It wasn't until the last 50 miles, when we entered Arizona and headed toward the Grand Canyon, that the scenery began to morph into burnt-orange, pink, and red mountain landscapes with feathery green pine trees, a welcome break for my eyes and spirit. I rolled down the window and took in the clean, crisp air.

Stefanie and Dave were waiting for us at Mather Campground. Stef, as I liked to call her, had a tearful reunion with Loren, whom she had once fostered until Loren wore out her welcome by almost eating Stef's cat on Christmas morning.

"Oh, Loren, I missed you, sweet girl," Stef said as Loren licked the tears off her face. With her bright red hair, alabaster skin, and sparkling blue eyes, Stef looks like an innocent Nordic nymph until you spot her many tattoos and realize she might be slightly wild, which only adds to her appeal.

Since I am mechanically challenged, Dave went to work pitching our tent. Our camping spot was shaded, private, and conveniently close to the restroom, where I took Loren in with me. As we came out, we encountered a woman with a leashed Chihuahua and miniature Pinscher who yapped ferociously at Loren, who just looked at them, startled, and kept going.

"It's always the ones with a 'good' reputation, huh?" said a young man who observed the scene. I laughed and nodded my head.

Dave and Stef were right next door to our campsite and came prepared with coolers full of food and drink. For dinner, they prepared a fantastic mixed grill of fresh salmon, chicken, zucchini, onions, and yellow squash, lightly seasoned and slightly smoky from the campfire stove.

All of us fed Loren little bits of meat as she sat patiently by the picnic table. She wasn't an obvious beggar, more of a strategic actress, scooting almost imperceptibly closer until you could no longer ignore her Little Orphan Annie routine. This consisted of eyes that grew as big as saucers and stared longingly into yours as she leaned against your legs. It was pretty hard to resist.

After dinner, we sat around the campfire, watching the stars, relaxing and catching up, me with a hot chocolate, Stef and Dave enjoying a beer, Loren laying on a blanket near the flames. "I've decided, I love camping… if someone else does the work," I proclaimed with a smile.

The next morning, I was not feeling the love. Our air mattress had sprung a leak, deflating completely by the middle of the night, the hard ground painful on my 40-year old hips. I threw down some extra blankets and tried to make the best of it. Loren was a trooper, snuggling up to me, which was easy to do in our tight, two-man tent, snoring contentedly. She didn't bark once, even though coyotes had been out in full force, baying for what seemed like hours. Loren only lifted her red and white head briefly when she heard the racket, then would settle back down with a sigh.

Slightly groggy the next morning, we awoke to the smell of bacon and eggs emanating from Stef and Dave's campground. I declined their kind offer to partake and instead ate my usual breakfast of Grape Nuts, though I did take Stef up on some freshly cut banana and apple slices. I didn't want to tackle the canyon with an overstuffed belly.

9

It was hot, in the 90s, so I donned shorts and a T-shirt for our trip to the Grand Canyon. The parking lot was crowded with cars bearing license plates from all over the country and tour groups were being dropped off from huge charter buses. We made our way through the masses to a paved trail along the South Rim.

"I've got it made in the shade!"

We barely moved ten yards before Loren decided she needed a break from the blaring sun. She planted herself in the shade and made her first friends of the day, a five year-old girl and her younger brother.

"Can we pet your dog?" the girl asked politely, looking from me to her parents.

"Sure," I said. They bent down and tentatively stroked Loren, who loved the attention.

"That's great, honey, you should always ask before petting a strange dog," the mom said with a smile. "She's a sweet doggy, huh?" The kids nodded.

"She's a pit bull," I said and the mom raised her eyebrows, pausing for a second.

"Well, she's a really good girl," the mom said and smiled. Score one for Loren.

Loren wasn't the only dog on the trail. There was a schnauzer and a big, black Afghan, who must have been really suffering under all that fur. Loren ignored them both, intent on the trail smells, way more into humans than other canines.

During another Loren-mandated break, we were approached by two young men from Phoenix. Soon enough, Loren was kissing all over one of them.

He told us of co-workers who had nailed a kitten inside a window frame and board, which he immediately set free and reported to his supervisors. I involuntarily gasped, looking over at Stef, who was equally disgusted. I know stuff like this happens all the time, but it never fails to shock me. He wanted to adopt a dog like Loren, had he not lived in an apartment. I suggested a cat.

Next came a senior couple that lived near Little Rock, Arkansas, whose 12-year old pit bull was lounging in the car, exhausted from an earlier hike. They told us their city has an ordinance banning pit bulls and that a police officer had threatened to confiscate their dog while they were shopping at a local farmer's market one day.

"Over my dead body," the lady told the officer, who, thankfully, let her take the dog home, with the admonition that she keep the dog undercover. Now they don't even take the chance of walking their beloved pet around the block for fear of being turned in.

***

Breed-specific legislation, or BSL, is currently enacted in approximately 300 towns across America. The term defines any law, ordinance or policy which pertains to a specific dog breed, but does not affect any others. Most commonly these are legal restrictions or prohibitions on the breeding and ownership of certain breeds.

In 1989, Denver, Colorado became the first city to launch BSL against pit bulls when three-year-old Fernando Salazar was killed by a pit bull after wandering into a neighbor's yard in 1986, followed by the 1989 mauling of Rev. Wilbur Billingsley, who sustained more than 70 bites and two broken legs after encountering a pit bull in an alley behind his home.

While BSL can start with allowing owners to keep their current dogs as long as they have them sterilized and carry liability insurance, Denver's was an outright ban that gave animal control officers the right to take pit bulls from their owners and bring them to a shelter, where they were killed (the only other option for owners was to move out of the city altogether or engage in lengthy, expensive court battles to prove their dogs were not pit bulls). Often, tips came from neighbors, who turned in dogs they suspected were pit bulls.

Since 1989, Denver has killed nearly 3,500 owned dogs believed to be pit bulls (not including pit bulls brought in as strays to shelters).

"It's discrimination, that's what it is," said Ed Fritz, campaign director of Pit Bulls: Saving America's Dog at Best Friends Animal Society in Kanab, Utah. "Most commonly it's a knee-jerk reaction by politicians who pander to constituents without knowing the facts."

Best Friends is the nation's largest non-profit animal welfare organization, with a no-kill rescue facility that houses more than 1,700 homeless pets awaiting adoption. They targeted saving pit bulls in 2008 as one point of a four-pronged approach to reduce the number of shelter-euthanized homeless pets. (The other points include the sterilization of feral cats, closing puppy mills, and First Home, Forever Home, which provides resources to financially strapped owners so they may keep their pets.)

"When Best Friends started in the 80s, the nation was killing about 18 to 20 million homeless pets a year. Then the animal welfare movement got rolling and with new approaches, we got the number to 4 to 6 million, but it's been stagnant there for the last decade," Fritz said. "We took a look and realized a large part of the reason came down to cats and pit bulls not getting out of the shelters alive."

Using their considerable clout and resources, Best Friends is focusing on creating changes at the legislative level, offering legal resources to targeted cities facing BSL and placing lobbyists to fight for the cause throughout the country.

"We're doing pretty good. In the last few months, we've helped defeat BSL in 22 to 23 communities. We've lost four," Fritz said.

Best Friends partnered with The National Canine Research Council in 2009 to launch a website calculation tool that uses census data to determine how much it will cost a particular city to enact BSL. It is estimated that out of 72.1 million dogs in the U.S., there are currently five million pit bulls or pit bull mixes, or approximately seven percent.

Apply that ratio to New York City, for example, where there are more than 1.5 million dogs, and the number of pit bulls is estimated at more than 106,000. To enact a breed ban there would cost taxpayers approximately $13 million a year, including enforcement, kenneling, veterinary care, euthanasia, disposal, DNA testing, and legal fees.

Alternatives to BSL include enforcement of leash laws, one-bite rules, and qualifying scales to determine a dog's aggressiveness, putting the responsibility on owners rather than a specific breed. Fritz noted that local animal welfare organizations can be instrumental in helping pit bull owners, especially in low-income areas, whether it's fixing a fence, providing training, or educating as to why it's dangerous to keep dogs chained.

"Our goals are the same, we want a safe and humane community for all," Fritz said. "To target a species based on breed is ludicrous. I tell people, if this were wrong, if pit bulls were really the culprit of this kind of danger, we wouldn't be putting the time and energy into protecting them."

One of the many problems with breed-specific legislation is how the dogs are determined to be pit bulls. Groups such as dogsbite.org (which declined to be interviewed for this book) state clearly on their website that "in the 3-year period of 2006 to 2008, pit bull type dogs killed 52 Americans and accounted for 59% of all fatal attacks. Combined, pit bulls and rottweilers accounted for 73% of these deaths."

Where did dogsbite.org get these statistics? You have to dig around for their source, but it's finally revealed on a downloadable PDF. "Information was gathered for this report through media accounts that were available at the time of the attack or found through Internet archives, including Google News Archive and AccessMyLibrary."

That's precisely the problem, said Karen Delise, president of the National Canine Research Council and author of *The Pit Bull Placebo.*

Delise started researching fatal dog attack statistics after seeing the rise in pit bulls being banned and killed in shelters due to their bad reputations. Many pit bull owners had called Delise, concerned and confused as to why their beloved breed was in such a state of siege.

She began with Center for Disease Control mortality tables for the last decade, pulling out any records that were coded as dog bite fatalities. From there, Delise would investigate each case by its accompanying veterinary or animal control records or other pertinent legal documents.

"I came into this breed neutral," Delise said. "I try to be very fair. Some people call me a pit bull apologist, but this is not only my personal feeling, this is what research bears out."

What she found was that only 13 out of 245 cases had absolute breed proof, through AKC records or DNA testings; 28 cases were based on visual identification agreed upon by a group that included animal control, veterinarian, law enforcement, and/or the dog's owner.

The rest of the cases, according to Delise, were based on conflicting reports - for example, what animal control determined as a pit bull/Labrador mix was reported as a straight pit bull in the media.

"There was no proof or consensus among animal professional as to what the dog was," Delise said. "Even I was surprised by these numbers."

Since there are approximately 25 breeds that resemble pit bulls, including boxers, mastiffs, Staffordshire terriers, and American bulldogs, visual identification is often unreliable. Bully breeds weren't the only victims of this process, either.

"Huskies, malamutes, and shepherds have so many cousins or closely related breeds, it's hard to say. One person can say husky, one can say malamute," Delise said. "If there's no consensus, you can't just pick one."

In some bite cases, the dog in question had disappeared altogether, though that doesn't stop the media from reporting their breed, especially if it's possibly a pit bull. This adds fuel to the fire of groups such as dogsbite.org, as Delise illustrated.

"There are cases where the dog is never captured, yet it's listed as a pit bull. What do you say to this?" Delise said. "These groups have an agenda and they use the media to support that agenda. Even in cases where animal control seizes and euthanizes the dog, then comes out and says the dog was a mixed breed, not a pit bull, they'll say it's a cover up. They completely disregard animal professionals, who clearly have no agenda for saying whether a dog is a pit bull or not."

As Delise outlined in *Pit Bull Placebo*, the tone of news coverage has changed over the last few decades. In the first part of the 20th century, reporters would include events leading up to the attack, such as a child disturbing a canine mother who had just given birth or teasing a chained dog. Since the 1980s, however, the headlines generally state "pit bull attack" with no background as to how the altercation came to pass.

"How did we skip over recognized canine behavior to breed behavior? How does it teach us to say it's a pit bull bite rather than a mother protecting her puppies?" Delise said. "Why are victims of pit bull attacks the only ones who get political, public, and media attention, but not if you're attacked by a German Shepherd or Labrador? On so many levels it's wrong...it doesn't solve the problem or help us understand it."

The specific problem with pit bull and pit bull mix attacks, as Delise illustrated, is usually created by a set of circumstances unique to the breed. Favored by a low-income demographic that uses them as protection or enforcement, pit bulls are often chained, unsocialized, neglected, and/or abused. Some are even trained to attack.

"Whether it's an Akita, Golden Retriever, Rottweiler, or pit bull, the family dog that sits at your feet and is taught how to behave appropriately, one that receives affection and guidance from its owners, doesn't wake up one morning and kill somebody. It just doesn't," Delise said. "If you pull back the curtains, you'll find all kinds of ugly stuff in their environment before a dog does something like that."

So why is America fixated on pit bulls? Why do they make headlines across the country, usually accompanied by a snarling, vicious photo?

"The only thing I can think of is that this taps into some kind of primal fear of predators. It's part of our nature, we love to be entertained by this kind of stuff and the media knows it," Delise said. "The pit bull is an advertising gimmick that's worked very well for them, but in real life, it's done horrific damage to the dogs and their owners, whether they're pit bulls or just look like them."

***

The sunset on the south rim was incredible that night, the sky a swirl of blue, gold, green, and pink against the red rocks. Dave and Stefanie hugged while watching the spectacle. I bent down and sat with my arm around Loren, who rewarded me with a lick on the nose. All of us grew quiet in the face of that magnificence.

Back at the campground, we were joined by Dan from New Jersey, a 60-ish engineer who had recently lost his job of 30 years and was heading to

Tucson for a wedding and to figure out his new place in the world along the way. His campsite was next to Dave and Stef. Though they had been introduced that morning to Loren's delight, that night, as Dan approached, she got very assertive, growling and pulling against her lead, her hair standing up on end around her scruff.

"I'm so sorry," I said to Dan, trying to calm Loren down. "I've never seen her like this."

"It's OK, she doesn't know me and it's dark," Dan said. He came over slowly and bent down, holding his hand to Loren. She sniffed it and slowly resumed her usual submissive demeanor, letting Dan pet her and eventually even licking his hand.

Stef looked at me with a grin and a shrug. "You know, it's a good thing that Loren's protective, Michelle," she said. "You have a lot of miles alone together. She's your bodyguard!"

"I know. It's weird to see her like that, but I'm kind of glad, too," I said.

It was true. Though I knew Loren to be a total softie, I also knew her appearance was imposing to certain people. That she could back it up gave me a certain level of security. We were heading to a series of strange places, mostly by ourselves.

Our bon voyage from Mather Campground the next morning was highlighted by an impromptu visit from a deer foraging in the low-hanging branches of the trees in our camp as we ate breakfast. Loren was very curious about the intruder, her floppy ears at full alert, her head cocked, straining at the end of her 20' lead wrapped around the table, until the deer gracefully leapt away.

We bid adieu to Stef and Dave and headed to Albuquerque. I was sad to lose the human camaraderie, but excited at the prospect of a real roof over our heads and a nice, long, hot shower.

As usual, Loren slept much of the way in the back cab. If I looked back or made a sound, she would pop open one amber eye and stare at me lazily. Sometimes she'd come up front and hang out with me before falling asleep, using the stick shift as a sort of pillow, which could not have been very comfortable, but I appreciated the company.

One thing kept Loren from being the perfect travel companion. She couldn't drive. Those miles could be tiring, especially on long desert highways, though the sparkling blue sky and puffy clouds set against red mountains gave my eyes a pleasant distraction from the endless asphalt, as did some retro ads along the road. Some of the highway billboards are from the 1950s or 60s, outdated signs that advertise Kodak film, along with various Southwestern knick knacks and attractions like Indian hieroglyphs and caves.

We bypassed them all and headed straight for our motel. Upon entering our room, we saw a family with a small Chihuahua, who looked at Loren in fear. "I think she's a pit bull," they whispered to one another and quickly closed their door. I wanted to run over with a postcard and introduce Loren, but I figured they wouldn't be receptive.

Sleeping in until 8 a.m. the next day was a real luxury, considering how tired I was and that I usually get up at 5:30 a.m. everyday in real life to walk my dogs. Since Loren doesn't need a middle of the night bathroom break, like I do, it wasn't a problem for her. As a matter of fact, I had to nudge her out of bed.

As we headed out that morning, we met the motel's maintenance manager, who came over to pet Loren. Turned out he had two pits and used to work at an Albuquerque shelter, which he couldn't do for long when dogs he cared for would be killed.

"Pits are the best dogs. It just breaks my heart to see so many put down," he said. "Wanna hear something classic? I've only been bit once by a dog. It was a little dog, like a Chihuahua or something. It attached itself to my calf and wouldn't let go."

After a Starbucks green tea and lemonade, I was feeling way more frisky, so we drove to a 9 a.m. A.A. meeting in the city, where I found a great shady parking spot for the hour so Loren would be comfortable. With eight years of sobriety, I knew it was important for me to regularly attend meetings, especially since I was out of my element. Connecting with other sober alcoholics kept my spirit in check and a drink far out of my hand.

There was a bearded man, a biker type, sleeping on the bench outside the meeting that made me a little nervous, so I checked on Loren every 15 minutes, happy to escape the smoke-filled room, which is something one rarely if ever experiences in California anymore.

After the meeting, another scruffy character, wearing a white wife-beater and dirty jeans, called after me when he saw Loren sitting in the front seat of the truck. "Cool dog. What's her name?"

"Loren," I replied. "Wanna meet her?"

"Yeah," he said.

An eager Loren jumped out of the truck and beelined for the guy, who was kneeling in anticipation. Loren leaned up against him and administered the first of several kisses.

"She's not my dog," I said.

"Really?" he asked.

"Nope. She lives at a no-kill shelter I volunteer at," I said. "We're traveling across country to promote pit bull awareness and homeless pet adoption. Are you online?"

"Yeah," he said.

I handed him a postcard and he perused it quietly.

"That's really cool," he said finally. "I love pits. There was one chained up down the street and I just couldn't stand it anymore, so I snuck in and set him free one day. I figured he had a better chance on the streets, maybe someone would take him in."

I sighed and nodded, not quite knowing what to say. The shelter isn't the best place for any dog, really, especially pit bulls, so I hoped the man was right, that the dog had found a nice person or family to call his own.

Loren and I cruised downtown Albuquerque, which reminded me of a Southwest Portland, a little rough around the edges, a place where funky shops and cute little adobe houses were mixed in among more traditional suburban architecture. The freeway overpasses were painted peach and blue for Southwestern flair.

I checked out my *Lonely Planet* guide for activities in Albuquerque and found the Petroglyph National Monument, where we arrived around noon. We hiked only about a half-mile of the one and a half-mile trail, since a lady with three border collies had warned us at the start that the sand got really hot the higher you travel. It was already in the high 80s or low 90s.

Loren, of course, was panting after just a short time and seeking shade wherever she could find it, which was sparse in that terrain. Knowing that snakes and other critters liked cool spots, I didn't like her hanging out there. Since we had seen a few petroglyphs, or rough ancient drawings etched on stone, I figured our mission had been accomplished. We hightailed it out of there.

Funny, people think pits are such big, tough dogs, but they're really rather delicate creatures. Loren's very fair on her nose, which chaps easily, and has light pink skin under her sparse fur, especially around her belly, which is practically naked. She much preferred the coolness of an air-conditioned room to roughing it outside.

For dinner, I checked on Yelp.com for Southwestern food and found the highly recommended Garcia's Restaurant right down the road. Best of all, they had a drive-thru, so I didn't have to leave Loren in the car for any length of time. It was so hot, I would've just run in for take out, but even that made me uncomfortable.

I ordered the red chili with beef and a bag of sopapillas. I broke into the latter on the drive back to the hotel. They were little triangles of lightly fried dough, like a thick, slightly crunchy sweet tortilla. Delish. How could something so simple be so good? I was thankful for all that bread to soak up the chili, a spicy fire-engine red concoction. This wasn't the Tex-Mex chili I was used to. This was more like straight pepper sauce with a few bits of meat and potatoes thrown in. Whew. It didn't make me breathe fire, but the aroma alone could clear your sinuses.

As I took Loren on her nightly potty break, we had an unexpected introduction to the Chihuahua and his family at the hotel. They didn't have him on a leash, so the little dog came barreling toward Loren, barking and snarling, coming within a foot of her.

Unbelievably, Loren not only shied away from the obnoxious "Pepe," she jumped up like a cartoon character that had just seen a mouse. She stood shaking next to me as his family screamed for Pepe to return. He did and they all jumped in their car and drove off, without apologizing or acknowledging what a great dog Loren was for not eating their ill-behaved Pepe, which she would have had every right to do out of self-defense.

Thank God she didn't. I wasn't sure what the laws were in Albuquerque, but I was pretty sure that if it came down to a pit bull versus a Chihuahua, Loren, despite being provoked and on a leash, would've lost, especially in the court of public opinion.

Everything's Bigger in Texas

A desert rainstorm was the night's entertainment, the thunder giving way to silver bolts of lightning against a black sky. I opened the window shade and the door to watch the show. At first, Loren was curious and joined me, but once a crack of thunder let loose, she ran from me to the security of the king-sized bed. After a few minutes, I closed up our room and joined her. Pretty soon, we were both snoring against the sound of raindrops lightly pelting the rooftop.

We took off from Albuquerque and headed to Amarillo, Texas, fortified by a fat carne adovada, or pork chunks cooked in spicy red sauce, breakfast burrito from Garcia's, which kept me full until way past lunchtime, a good thing on a long drive. The landscape out of New Mexico to Texas morphed from a picturesque Southwestern desert of red rock into flatlands of dry, beige scrub for miles, the sky bright blue and unencumbered by any vertical scenery until farm houses and silos began to appear, along with pasture land and cows. Black ones. Striped ones. Spotted ones. Tan ones. A few with horns. They silently went about their business as we went whizzing by.

Amarillo is a mid-sized suburb, unremarkable really, with hotel chains and big box stores lining the highways. Our motel was a two-story 50s throwback on a main road, adjacent to the highway, a bit musty, but comfortable. I searched for a nearby park to take a stroll with Loren, as wandering alongside a major thoroughfare is far from relaxing.

Wimberly Park was lush, green, and set in a quaint neighborhood of ranch-style brick houses, where I spotted more than one set of neighbors actually speaking with one another (for some reason, this is a rarity in Southern California). Loren went on a sniffing mission, especially when she saw or smelled several families barbecuing their lunch. She tried, unsuccessfully, to drag me over for a meet and greet. Instead, we settled for a brief break in the grass, which was dry and cushy on my road-weary rear.

When we returned to the hotel, the wind blew the only copy of my road itinerary around in the parking lot as I frantically searched for the room key. I chased down the pages and managed to retrieve all but one, but never found the key. My phone rang. It was Wayde.

My boyfriend, God love him, had just moved us all in to his new home four days before Loren and I left for our trip. He is a cat person and his fluffy calico Sugar Butt, or Sugar B as we call her, is old and mellow, typically napping most of the day away. Wayde was not used to the antics of two lively dogs. He was in the middle of a huge construction job, too, not to mention remodeling our house, and just a little stressed out. He was missing me and I him.

Following our brief conversation, I headed back to the front desk for a replacement key, then lugged my computer equipment into our room, followed by Loren, who quickly settled on the bed, where I had thrown some of our stuff before turning on the computer and checking my email. Within seconds, there was an odd sound behind me, the crunching of plastic. Loren was eating my cell phone charger.

For the first time, I wanted to be home. Forget these strange motel rooms and stranger people, this strange dog who had taken a liking to eating expensive electronic equipment.

"Loren!" I said, pulling shards of plastic from her mouth, checking her throat with my fingers, then shaking my head in frustration. Thankfully, I had caught her before she had the chance to swallow any.

I sighed deeply and sat on the edge of the bed. Loren looked a bit sheepish. I gave her a half smile and felt for my favorite part underneath her chin, where a wrinkled wattle of soft velveteen fur resided, and stroked it for a minute. She stretched out and offered me her belly for a rub. All was forgiven.

Thinking a good BBQ dinner might be the cure to what ailed me, we hopped in the truck and headed down the road a few miles to Dyer's BBQ, which not only shared Wayde's last name, but was highly recommended in the book *Roadfood* by Jane and Michael Stern, which became my culinary bible on the road.

I found a nice shady spot in the front of the restaurant where I could leave Loren in the truck and make frequent checks on her. Loren was used to living in an outdoor kennel in 105-110 degree weather during the summer, and it was probably in the high 70s or low 80s here, but I wanted to make sure she would be comfortable and safe.

I needn't have worried. Once she was set up with her blanket, water bowl, and plenty of ventilation through the cracked windows, Loren couldn't have been happier. She probably craved some alone time, too.

Meanwhile, I got to take a break from Styrofoam'd meals eaten in motels to enjoy a peaceful respite in the Western-themed dining room, accompanied by a good magazine. There were red and white checkered cloths on the table, warm wood throughout, and a friendly, mellow vibe. For $6.95, I got the "light" dinner with two ribs, potato salad, onion rings, coleslaw, beans, and bread. Don't even ask what the regular meal comes with. Everything truly is bigger in Texas.

The ribs were smoky, meaty, falling-off-the-bone tender, the onion rings light and crisp, the potato salad and coleslaw stellar takes on the classics.

Satiated, I picked up a T-shirt for Wayde on my way out as a token of my appreciation.

***

The trip to Flower Mound, a suburb outside of Dallas where my cousin Pat Amick and his family live, was peaceful, endless fields of wheat swaying before returning to the green pasturelands I had become accustomed to. We passed the Texas Motor Speedway, a mile-long concrete compound with bleachers and outbuildings that seemed to touch the cloudless sky. Wayde's a Nascar fan, but I'm not. From the size of the track, it seems I'm in the minority.

Pat's wife Stacey greeted us as if we were long lost buddies when, in reality, it was the first time we'd met. Pat and I had become fast friends after meeting 15 or so years ago, when my father was united with his biological father (which is Pat's and my grandfather), but we hadn't seen each other in at least a decade. I gave this woman a lot of credit, welcoming me and a strange dog, a pit bull no less, with open arms. She even put their family cat up at the vet's for the night.

Stacey was an ER nurse before she became a full-time mom and ran her household with authoritative efficiency, taking calls, making calls and coordinating our trip to Operation Kindness, a no-kill shelter in Carrollton, as Loren and I made ourselves comfortable for a few minutes. The Amick house was a new brick two-story with Mediterranean/Tuscan décor. Loren and I were staying in the den, with an olive chenille couch that pulled out into a bed, a nice break from the bright colors and hyper-tropical patterns of our budget motel rooms.

Loren and I walked with Stacey through the upper-middle class neighborhood to pick up Leslie, 10, and Sean, 8, from their school just up the road, enjoying the soft carpet of lawn, which blanketed the well-landscaped neighborhood, underneath our feet. Stacey went to retrieve the kids across the street while Loren and I took a break on the grass, shaded by a leafy tree.

Within minutes, the Amick kids, both blonde-haired, blue-eyed cuties, were bounding toward us, excited to meet their Aunt Michelle, but even more interested in her travel companion.

"Hi Loren," Leslie said as she dropped her bags to lean down and pet her. Loren responded with a kiss. Sean, who is autistic, kept more of a distance as throngs of kids and their parents passed by in a wave of after-school commotion. Loren was calm throughout. I was very proud of her.

Girl Scout Troop 1604, which both Leslie and Stacey belong to, met us immediately afterwards at Stacey's house so we could drop off donations to Operation Kindness. The troop had a donation drive on May 9 at a local

PetSmart, collecting over $500 in items and gift cards in less than two hours as part of their Journey Award service project.

Following the caravan of SUVs to Operation Kindness, my heart leapt in panic as we approached the I-35 overpass to Carrollton. The slim strip of concrete lurched upward and looked like its ultimate destination was heaven. I looked at Loren and shook my head.

"Holy shit, Loren," I told her in a somber tone. "I don't know about this."

But I didn't have a choice. After paying a toll, the caravan shot out to the off ramp and I had no idea how to find an alternate route, so, heart in my throat, we paid the toll and made our ascent, me praying the whole way. It was like being on a roller coaster with no chain holding me in place. Visions of plummeting off the side began to fill my brain before I got a grip and focused on a more positive outlook, making it to whatever was on the other side of that concrete terror.

"Stay calm, you can do this, stay calm, you're fine," I told myself, taking short shallow breaths, like I imagined one does in labor, as I gripped the steering wheel.

It felt like forever before the overpass began its descent downward to the adjoining freeway and leveled off to a flat, uneventful road once more. I exhaled deeply and slowly, following the caravan into the parking lot of Operation Kindness.

"Oh my God, you Texas chicks are crazy!" I said to Stacey and one of the other Girl Scout mothers. "That was gnarly. I was scared out of my mind."

Stacey laughed and shrugged. "Piece of cake," she said with a wink.

The Girl Scouts began pulling bags of food, boxes of treats, and assorted toys out of the SUVs and brought their haul into the facility's front lobby. With its shiny linoleum floors, brightly colored walls, and gleaming picture windows, Operation Kindness looked more like a high-end veterinary office than a shelter.

A pen filled with fluffy puppies quickly caught the girls' attention. Simultaneously they draped their lanky bodies over the metal to reach down and pick up the pups, cooing and petting them before we were led by Nancy, Operation Kindness' lead volunteer, into a large, open room filled with cats, where many languidly stretched on carpeted posts as the girls petted them.

At any given time, Operation Kindness has more than 200 dogs and cats available for adoption. There are 42 paid staff members and more than 500 volunteers on their roster, so the animals get exercise and attention daily, going for walks on the park-like grounds or hanging out and playing in large runs.

Nancy told me that the most common types of dogs at Operation Kindness are lab mixes and the indoor kennel area bore that out, filled with friendly chocolate, black, and yellow labs of all ages. There were a few pit bull and shepherd mixes, too, as well as some very cute little Jack Russell and Chihuahua types. (People who aren't in rescue always seem surprised that there are adorable small dogs or puppies available at their local shelter or rescue; trust me, there

"Think they'll make me an honorary Girl Scout?"

are. There is no good reason to buy from a breeder or pet store).

Fortunately, Operation Kindness has an incredible adoption rate of 90% or more and as a no-kill facility, like The Brittany Foundation, the animals have a home for life there if they don't find a family of their own.

After our tour, the Operation Kindness ladies came out to meet Loren, and pose for a photo. They were extremely grateful for the donations, which as a non-profit, they rely on to operate.

I was so impressed with the Girl Scouts - it was encouraging to see young people becoming aware and involved in the plight of shelter animals. Maybe their generation or the following would finally achieve a truly humane society with no more homeless pets.

***

The Texas night was cooling down and the Amicks wanted to take me to their favorite Italian place in town, complete with outdoor patio. Though their yard was fenced in by six-foot concrete walls, I was paranoid that Loren would somehow find a way out, so I put her on the 20-foot lead and looped it around a pillar. She look at me quizzically as we walked away, but as we piled into the car, I didn't hear any whining. A good sign.

Patrizio's, set in a massive strip mall, was everything the Amicks had promised. We gathered around a circular wrought iron and marble table and perused the menus. For me, it was the open-faced ravioli, thick ribbons of homemade pasta enveloped with garlic cream sauce, roasted artichokes, mushrooms, and peppers.

"You could cover anything in cream sauce and it would be good," Pat remarked to chuckles. He's a software engineer and still looks about 25.

Loren was fine when we came home, calm and unruffled. Leslie and Sean spent some time with us in the backyard as I encouraged Loren to do her business.

Sean started running around the backyard and Leslie joined in, which at first flustered Loren. Soon enough, she was bounding back and forth with the kids with an exuberance I'd rarely seen from her, weaving in and out from their legs. It scared me.

"Be careful. I don't want her to knock you over," I said. "Don't get her too excited."

"OK, don't be so dramatic, we've never had a dog before," Leslie said, slowing down, Loren standing next to her, tongue hanging out happily.

I apologized and tried to further explain my logic, but gave up. They are kids. I am a boring, overprotective adult.

Inside, Loren had a field day sniffing after the cat scent and developed an odd fixation with a cast-iron buffalo stationed on a coffee room table. "Chh, chh," Pat would say to her, touching her sides with pointed fingers, doing his best Cesar Millan impression. Loren quickly backed off, feeding Pat's latent *Dog Whisperer* ego.

Most of all, Loren loved Stacey and the kids, following them around well, like a puppy, leaning in for a snuggle whenever possible.

"You could adopt her, ya know," I told them.

"I wish we could," Stacey said softly with her faint Texas drawl. "I don't think our cat would like it, though."

Probably not.

When we departed the next morning, all the Amicks signed a paw print magnet and put it on the truck. I liked the idea that this family would be with us on the rest of our trip, at least in spirit.

***

Our next stop was Terrell, Texas to visit with my good friend Anita Rupe-Peters, who I've known since high school and hadn't seen in years. Her family rescued a male Aussie mix named Jaxson and although Loren doesn't show much interest in other dogs, and at times an outright dislike, I naively hoped she'd make a canine friend.

It was not to be. When I pulled up in front of Anita's house, a sprawling one-story set in the country, and let her out to greet Jaxson, who was behind their white picket fence, Loren's fur began to ruffle immediately and she snarled. My sweet girl.

Anita and I tried to walk the pair, but they were much more interested in a potential brawl then any scenery or smells ahead. It seemed our plans to stay overnight at Anita's would have to be amended. Luckily, I had 20 one night gift certificates for a pet-friendly motel chain that was kind enough to sponsor us, and they had a location in Terrell.

Before doing so, Anita, Zach, her 4-year old son and doppelganger, Loren and I decided to go to Subway for sandwiches to take to the park, piling in Anita's late model SUV, Loren in the back with Zach. The restaurant wasn't crowded, but the scene was utter chaos as two teenage girls, one overly enthusiastic and the other completely apathetic, took forever to make our sandwiches.

The unhappy cashier drew a total blank when I gave her gift cards for the purchase and proceeded to mix up our order with the customer behind us. I attempted to walk her through the situation, to no avail. Skinny and very pregnant with a bright red and black weave and scarlet talon-like fingernails, the girl gave us a long, blank silent stare before she simply walked away from the whole scene.

The sandwich maker took over and apologized. "She's in a bad way. Her house burned down, she's pregnant, and she doesn't know what she's going to do. She's in a bad way."

When we walked outside, the pregnant girl was sitting on a curb, her head in her hands. I said a quick prayer for her and vowed to remember this the next time I took a stranger's attitude personally. It usually has nothing to do with you.

Anita drove us to Kaufman Lakes, a sprawling park nearby. As the clouds gathered and added a heavy layer of humidity to the air, we ate our sandwiches and caught up.

"Any sandwich left, Zach?"

Growing up in Simi Valley, California, a predominantly white middle-class suburb famous for acquitting four Los Angeles Police Department officers in the Rodney King beating case, Anita and I had made friends through our older sisters in the ninth grade and remained close throughout high school, forming a tight trio with our other best friend Jill Howe-Vercos, now a psychologist, wife and mother living in Venice, California.

Anita, her husband James, and Zach moved to Texas a few years before. James, who works in both investment banking and information technology, had been laid off a few times since they moved, due to the recession. Times were tight, with Anita selling items she found at garage sales on Ebay or goat's milk soap she made by hand.

"Let's go for a walk around the lake," Anita suggested after we finished eating. It was getting toasty and I knew how Loren reacted to the heat, but figured it was worth a shot. Loren reluctantly got up off the cool concrete and we headed toward the half-foot high grass, which was a bit marshy in spots.

As we trudged along, Anita casually mentioned there were snakes near the lake. Black mambas or something poisonous, she added. Now, I may not be afraid of rodents or spiders, but say snake and I'm ready to run back to the car and drive far, far away to snake-less safety.

"I hate snakes, Anita," I said.

"Oh, don't be such a wimp. They're not going to get you," Anita replied.

"How do you know?" I asked as Anita rolled her eyes.

"They're just not, OK?" she said impatiently.

I spent the majority of our meant-to-be peaceful walk with an anxious eye out for slithering creatures, Anita giggling at my paranoia. Loren the hot dog was panting, taking breaks in the shade whenever she could, which upped my fear of her getting bit by a snake. Good times.

Still, it was beautiful. Texas has some mighty big sky and pretty country. I was lost in the scenery, my head in the huge puffy clouds, until I heard a sound coming out of the water's edge. Loren and I looked at each other, then Anita.

"That's a snapping turtle," Anita said matter-of-factly.

"OK, are there any nice reptiles in Texas? Ones that don't bite or snap or kill you?" I asked. "Yikes."

We went back to Anita's house to pick up my truck. She led us into town to find our motel. As we checked in, the clerk took my gift certificate, which wouldn't go through, and gave me a key until she could process the transaction. Moments later, I got a phone call in the room.

It was the clerk. "I need to see you up front," she said sternly.

Uh-oh. I grabbed my purse and went to the desk.

"These certificates are coming up invalid or stolen," she said.

Visions of languishing away in a squalid Texas jail, with poor Loren in the pound, went streaming through my head as I struggled to recount the names and info of the people who issued them to me. What would I do if Loren went to the shelter? What if they killed her? Oh my God. Would this end like a bad made-for-TV women's prison movie?

The clerk was patient and made the appropriate calls to corporate until the situation was resolved, but it was scary for a minute.

Stuff like this made me crazy. Plans going awry. Humidity and the threat of reptiles. Dogs not getting along. Being tired from endless driving. Missing home and the people that knew me. It was just day six and I was already beginning to wonder...was I insane for taking this trip? Or was it just Texas? Didn't Susan Sarandon say something like, "Nothing good happens in Texas" in *Thelma and Louise*?

As I attempted to relax and enjoy a dinner later on that evening at Anita's, Loren kept setting off the car alarm, causing me to cut short my visit with my old friend, but not before getting to take in an awesome Texas sunset.

***

Houston, we have a problem. That saying reverberated through my head as I drove up to our hotel, located in a gritty area downtown. That's the joy of making reservations online when you have no idea where you're going, you don't know where you're going to end up, a Shangri-la or a scary hood. This was the latter.

At least there were no problems checking in. The motel's corporate office had called in advance. I asked the 350-pound hotel clerk for a room near the office, explaining I was a woman traveling alone and all. For some unknown reason, I felt compelled to tell her about my trip. (It gets lonely on the road.) I even handed her a postcard.

"You know about pets then? Because my niece brought home a cat and I just don't know what to do with it," the woman said, her huge hazel eyes, the color reminiscent of Loren's, magnified through a pair of glasses. She had several tattoos, including one on her upper arm, barely visible against her black skin. Her hair was dyed a spectacular shade of orange.

"What do you want to know?" I asked, already getting nervous, anticipating this cat might end up in a shelter.

"Well, the cat just wants to boo boo everywhere and it's making a mess," she said.

I took boo boo as an euphemism for going to the bathroom.

"Well, do you have a cat box?" I asked.

"Yeah, but she doesn't like to use it," the clerk replied.

"Well, do you clean it?" I asked.

Blink, blink. Silence.

"Well, how often do I have to do that?" she finally asked.

"Well, you should clean it with a scoop at least every other day and then clean it completely once a week," I said.

Blink, blink. Silence.

"Oh," she said.

I shook my head and gave a half-hearted smile, not certain what to say next. There was a brief awkward silence.

"I had a dog once," she went on. "But that dog would just boo boo all over the carpet."

"Did you have a doggy door?" I asked.

Blink, blink.

"What's that?"

"A door that lets your dog in and out of the house," I said.

Blink, blink.

"Oh, no," she said. Silence. "Well, you have a nice stay in Houston."

I didn't have the heart to ask her what happened to the dog.

I consulted my trusty GPS, which I had named Gidget, for a nice place to take a stroll. My parents had bought Gidget for me so I wouldn't get hopelessly lost on the road. They know I have no sense of direction, unlike my father, who was born with an inner compass. Never tell me to go east or west. It's left, right or straight ahead in my world. Gidget was very gracious. She never got mad at me if I missed a turn. She'd just say "calculating route" in her melodious voice.

Loren and I went for a walk at TC Jester Park. At two in the afternoon, it was filled with disaffected white skateboarder boys and Goth girls, just like when I was a kid. A few teenagers nodded with a bit of respect as Loren and I wandered around. I heard one of them mumble, "Cool dog."

The scene at Yo Momma's Soul Food, where I decided to get takeout lunch, reminded me of *Animal House* when the white college kids enter the all-black nightclub to see Otis Day & The Knights. Disbelieving stares. Silence that burned my ears. Time that seemed to stand still for a few seconds.

It was a shock for me to be the minority, but I tried to affect an air of belonging, rather unconvincingly.

A lanky cook, standing behind a steaming buffet of comfort food in a stained apron and threadbare T-shirt, eyed me coolly. He wore his long braided locks in a tight hairnet, giving him a Snoop Dogg effect. The cashier, an older lady that could have been his mother, just raised an eyebrow as I tried to choose from some delectable looking items.

The cook was kind enough to walk me through my options. I paid, hurriedly grabbed my package and set off for the hotel, laughing at myself on the ride back. I was either brave or stupid, or maybe both.

It was worth it. The food was great. Succulent smothered pork chops, creamy macaroni and cheese with a little zing to it, perfectly cooked collard greens; only the corn was a disappointment, soggy and canned. The rest was the real deal and all of it was just $7.95. I licked off some of the gravy and shared my chop with Loren, who loved it, too. Then we took a nap.

After that caloric splurge, I was up for a healthy dinner, which was just what my cousin Elizabeth or "Eddy" Maxwell made for us that evening. She lived about 15 miles from the hotel, so once again I sucked it up to go over some wild overpasses, talking to Loren all the while for encouragement.

I had just met Eddy, Pat's sister, a few months back, when our Uncle Roger, my dad's brother, got married in California. Eddy's way cool - she likes alternative music, does media relations for a living, is into animal rescue and is about my age, so of course, we hit it off right quick.

Eddy had two sweet dogs, Simon and Sarah, each ten or so, both with a few health problems. She put her dogs outside and let Loren hang in with us. Loren was curious, as always, especially when she spotted Simon and Sarah outside. Wagging tail. Slightly ruffled fur. Maybe they would have gotten along...I didn't want to chance it, though. It wouldn't have been a fair fight had things gone awry.

We had a fantastic dinner of broiled snapper, homemade salsa, and a very beautiful salad with fresh peppers, cherry tomatoes, and homemade vinaigrette. Eddy is quite the cook, which I suspected when I saw her collection of Penzey spices on the counter. Anyone with bouquet garni in their spice rack isn't messing around.

It was so nice to have familiar human interaction along our stops, friends and family who really supported us on this trip. The hardest thing about traveling, minus the annoying inconveniences, is being alone. I mean, I had Loren, and she was awesome company for sure, and I'm kind of a lone wolf anyway, but it was still nice to see a friendly face here and there.

Some of the strangers we met were cool, too, such as the dog lovers who felt compelled to share their stories. Then you had the idiots like Pepe the Chihuahua's family. Thankfully, it had been more good than bad. Which is what I thought the world is like in general.

Or at least I did until we went to San Antonio.

***

The parking lot was alive with hip hop music, buff, tattooed men and even buffer dogs, like a concert, only instead of drinking beer and chatting up chicks, these guys were showing off their four-legged property. It was 10:45

a.m. and the American Bully Kennel Club show in San Antonio was just about to start.

The American Bully is a dog recognized by the United Canine Association, an all-breed registry for purebred canines, as purebred; the breed is not recognized by the American Kennel Club. According to the UCA, the American bully was created by breeders in the 1980s, who crossed American Pit Bull terriers with Staffordshire terriers. The result is what some people refer to as a "pit-o-patamus."

I was waiting behind a truck filled with these massive bullies, their block heads and cropped ears peeking up from a crate in back of the bed. There were white ones and black ones, marked ones and brindle ones with spiked collars being dragged in the parking lot by their owners. They had the same markings of the pit bulls I am used to, but were way stockier, stouter, lower to the ground, their heads about 50 percent larger, their faces more impassive than curious, most slobbering in the budding Texas heat.

Cars boasted stickers with names of kennels:Bullet Proof, Kountry Boys. In one case, an especially committed kennel had an elaborate mural painted on the back of their truck, immense bullies awash in swirls of color and intricate calligraphy.

I took a deep breath and grabbed my camera, not sure of how to play my role here. Should I be stealth, pretend I wanted to buy a dog and see where that led, or just be honest and say I was writing a book about pit bulls? I'm not a very good liar or actress, so it might be hard to pull off the innocent bystander routine, but would breeders be willing to talk to a rescuer, which I knew would come out within minutes of the conversation?

This I debated while in line, when a bully in front of me started throwing up clear bile. Its owner failed to take notice.

"Hey man, your dog is throwing up," someone casually said to the owner, a huge African American guy with short braids in a low ponytail.

"Huh?" He looked down, barely moving, as solid as an oak tree and just about as unyielding to movement.

"Do you want me to get him some water?" I asked, grabbing my keys and preparing to rush to my truck. I was glad I had taken Loren to a groomer for a spa day instead of trying to navigate her through this madness.

The human oak tree finally moved his dog out of line and brought him outside, where the bully promptly collapsed. With his owner rubbing its sides, looking blank, I ran to get water and Loren's bowl. When I got back, the dog had got back on its feet, but was still slobbering heavily. I poured some water, but he refused to drink.

"Here, you keep the bottle," I said and handed it to the man. "For later, if you need it."

"Thank you," the man said, almost imperceptibly. For a big guy, he sure was quiet. Maybe he liked to let his dog do the talking for him.

"No problem," I said.

After a minute, we both got back in line. Outside, families were unloading their vehicles, mostly trucks, taking out toddlers alongside dogs bigger than their strollers. White, Hispanic, black, it was a genuine multicultural affair, with one look generally dominating for the men. Hip hop gangster, with low slung pants or shorts, graphic T-shirts, hats turned to the side or back, and tattoos up and down arms, on necks, even underneath eyes.

For women, the style was either soccer mom or hoochie mama, with lots of bling, low-cut shirts, and in one case, laced up high-heeled boots paired with short shorts. For some families, it was matching outfit time, with babies to grandmas sporting colorful T-shirts emblazoned with their kennel name.

Inside the convention center, it was pandemonium. Tupac and Dr. Dre boomed and a swirl of attendees crowded vendor booths hawking everything from thick leather collars studded with five-inch spikes to puppies as young as eight weeks old.

The smell was familiar to anyone who's ever been to a large, confined adoption event. Musk, plus a mixture of urine and disinfectant and perhaps a touch of canine fear, except this was stronger than anything I'd previously been exposed to.

Dogs were paired up in cages and crates, some with barely enough or no room to turn around. Stacked from largest to smallest, the breeders showcased puppies, most with cropped ears and spiked collars, on top. Poop and urine stains were smeared across the floor, something that would never be tolerated at the adoption fairs I'd been to.

Bigger is better

An American Bully

There must have been 50 or more breeders there and their status was apparent, like most conventions, by the size of their graphics and amount of technology in their booths. Some spaces had small, stark two-color banners and a few business cards strewn about, while others had floor to ceiling, full color banners and video displays, as well as plush, carpeted platforms where the breeders would pull out the dogs and proudly hold up their improbable heads with thick, heavy chains.

Even when I would try to be discreet and take candid shots of the crowd, if any of these guys caught me, they would immediately stop themselves and assume the position, crouching over and pulling their dog's head up, then looking up themselves, macho pride spreading to the corners of their mouths and their eyes.

I came across a man holding a big brindle male. Most of the dogs present seemed to be males, their balls intact, of course. What the hell, I thought, and approached the owner.

"I'm writing a book about pit bulls. Do you mind if I ask you a few questions?" I said, reporter's notepad in hand for credibility.

Instead of being reticent, Roderick of Smash That Kennels in Houston was more than happy to talk to me. He was there with his sons, ranging in ages from four to teenage, and professed to be an avid pit bull lover.

"I've never fought a dog. My stomach couldn't take it," he said. "I've just always had pit bulls. They never bit anyone. A lot is in raising them."

Roderick started breeding Razor's Edge bullies, a very popular bloodline, about five years ago.

"We try to keep the bloodline exclusive. We don't breed all willy nilly. We breed for temperament. We wouldn't breed Petron," he nodded to the huge beast by his side, "to anyone with an aggressive female."

Smash That Kennels breeds about six pups per year, which sell for up to $2,500 apiece, and also provides stud service with dogs like Petron for $1,000 or more.

"That's nothing," Roderick said. "Petron's grandpa on his mom's side, I heard some dude paid $65,000 for him."

According to Roderick, he does background checks on people who want to purchase his puppies and makes them sign a contract that requires a follow up in six months. He doesn't see a connection that breeding bullies might take away the potential adoption of a pit bull from a shelter, where hundreds of thousands are killed every year.

"The type of people that buy my dogs aren't going to go to the shelter. They know what they want and they can get it here," he said.

Still, Roderick has a soft spot for the type of pit bulls he grew up with and wants to open a no-kill rescue someday, to get them rehabilitated and adopted out into good homes.

Ezekiel of Army of God Kennels in Mesquite, Texas is another contradiction, a breeder who rescues stray pit bulls and tries to find them homes while simultaneously producing up to 36 puppies per year, which he sells for $1,500 to $2,500 each.

He trains all his dogs, which live either in his home or with relatives, rather than in kennels, and takes them to schools and parks to educate people about the breed.

"Bullies aren't mean, they're real sweet," Ezekiel said.

He not only requires a contract from adopters, with a clause that they must spay or neuter the puppies, he won't sell to single men.

"I don't want them to go to fighters or backyard breeders trying to make money," Ezekiel said.

When I asked how he felt about producing puppies when there are so many dogs dying in shelters, Ezekiel paused for a moment.

"I don't really see it that way, but you bring up a good point. If I have a litter that doesn't sell, that dog won't get rebred. I won't keep rebreeding. I don't see the point in doing that," he said.

As we spoke, a small, fawn-colored female was resting by Ezekiel's side. Her name was Guera and despite her obvious sweetness, she was given an intimidating look via cropped ears and a collar with three-inch spikes.

Ezekiel, a young active duty military man, Iraq veteran, and father of a three year-old daughter, began breeding two years ago and felt that the name of his kennel has made inroads into reaching a culture that might need to hear a little more about God.

"This is a huge diversity of people here, white, Mexican, black, and when they ask me why Army of God, I say why not? Who's the founder of us, who gave His life for us? Some of these guys are big time drug dealers or thugs and God has changed their life. I see it a lot. I see it making a difference in this community," he said.

The one female breeder I spoke to, Laura of Throwback Bullies and Bullyvard in New Mexico, began breeding four years ago and is now producing four to six litters a year from dogs like Raja, a smaller but still stout blue and white bully perched in the top cage in her booth.

"I'm not in it for the money, I'm in it for the dogs, to bring their reputation up to where it belongs," she said. "I hope we're making a difference by showing how you should raise a bully. It's about pairing good owners with good dogs."

Laura, too, makes owners sign a contract, though she admitted to shipping dogs to other states and even as far as Canada. When I asked how she controlled the application process when she couldn't meet the owners, she said Throwback Bullies does background checks on everyone they sell dogs to.

"We hope they won't be used for fighting. The starting price for our dogs is high. I can't imagine anyone paying $2,000 for a dog, then taking them to a fight," Laura said.

She was the one breeder who acknowledged that she could possibly be adding to the problem of pit bull overpopulation.

"I think about it every time we have a litter. It's a hard decision to make. These dogs are what's in right now. Ten years ago it was the gang style pits, the ones you find in shelters now," Laura said. "I hope it doesn't turn into a thousand rescues for bullies ten years from now."

I circled the auditorium, not sure where to go next, when I saw the banner for Atomic Dogg Magazine, the bible for bully breeders. The full color glossy magazine is published in Los Angeles and features profiles on breeders across the country, health care and training tips, as well as kennel ads that rival car magazines for cheesecake appeal, usually consisting of a scantily clad woman posing provocatively with a massive bully.

The first issue was published in April 2006 and according to Moses Nuno, Atomic Dogg's west coast representative, the magazine has grown in readership and advertising by 145 percent every year since. A tall, strapping Hispanic man, Moses was pleased to talk to me, chivalrously gesturing for me to sit on top of a crate, which was the only place to take a break in the booth, as he filled me in on the publication's history.

"When we first came out, Atomic Dogg didn't have a lot of ads or even pages. Now we feature a lot of celebrities like Sean Kingston and Lil John. It's attractive to everyone in our culture," Moses said. "We didn't have an outlet before, we were stereotyped as outcasts. We've come together so we have a community where we can talk to others with the same interest."

As we talked, one of Nuno's own dogs, a hulking, slobbering snow-white male, was led back to his crate, which was next to my makeshift chair. He remained listless throughout the entire exchange, as did most of the dogs I saw that day.

"These shows are getting huge, too," Moses continued, gesturing to the crowd around his booth. "We get two thousand or more people coming to each one, across the country. There's a lot of pride. Everyone wants to be the next champion. My slogan is 'Be biggest bully on the block.'"

Moses said that Atomic Dogg Magazine always sponsors a rescue at each show, such as the local humane society, and tries to host a rescue/shelter dog class competition whenever possible. The magazine also regularly runs stories on pit bull advocates like Tia Torres and Brandon Bond.

"We know how many pit bulls are at rescues. We try to do whatever we can," Moses said. "A lot of us have rescue dogs. I have one myself."

"So, if you know what's going on with pit bulls in shelters and rescues, how can you justify breeding?" I asked him.

"People are getting away from pit bull and going towards bullies. There's a big difference in the two dogs," he said. "Their structure, their temperament. American Bullies tend to be more on the nonchalant side. We personify and express ourselves through these dogs."

Nonchalant? It seemed to me these bullies had the most charming pitty characteristics, a zest for life and immense love of humans, bred right out of them, but I kept that to myself.

Instead, I asked, "Then why would you want to present such a threatening image by cropping their ears and putting big old spike collars on them?" Moses nodded his head as I spoke, taking in every word. "Isn't that going against bettering the bully image? That's what all the breeders keep telling me, but I don't see how this is any better than what's already out there."

He took a moment to answer. "People want their dog to be the toughest, to stand out in the crowd. It could be interpreted as the macho factor," Moses said. "We don't put big spikes on our dogs, but a lot of newbies like to. It's like how some people like to put a lot of chrome on their car. It's all about the look."

I thanked Moses for his time and got up. My head spun, overwhelmed by sensory overload. Why didn't these people see what they were doing was, in my opinion, very wrong, not only for creating a supply of dogs when millions die in shelters, but by creating a monstrous-looking breed that appeals to an element that wouldn't exactly further the reputation of the pit bull, if this demographic was typical of its fans and owners?

Lost in thought, I was pleasantly surprised when a young-looking woman with long brown hair and braces stopped me with a flyer and started in with how many pit bulls were dying in shelters and how her non-profit organization, Product Bull, was trying to help them by rescuing and rehabilitating homeless pit bulls and taking them into schools and libraries for humane education. Her name was Michelle Gustavo-Villareal and she was a former bully breeder who stopped the practice after three years, once she realized the negative impact it was having on potential adoptions.

"In Brownsville, where I live now, the shelter takes in 30 to 40 dogs a day and 70 percent of those are pit bulls, which are put down immediately or pulled only through rescue. Other dogs are given three days for adoption, but pit bulls aren't even given one hour. It's genocide," she said.

Michelle continued that she was trying to fight BSL in Brownsville and proposed the idea of licensing pit bull owners as a safety measure instead. She believed that the public needed to see the doctors, lawyers, grandmas and teachers that own and love pit bulls, not just the stereotypical gang-banger type so prevalent in popular culture.

"These people are all they see," she said, waving her arms to the crowd around us.

Michelle noted only about one out of 20 attendees at the show would stop and let her give the Product Bull spiel. "They don't care to listen," she said. "They're here to show dogs, gain points, and gain recognition. They're not here to re-educate the public on how beautiful the breed is."

Sure enough, the show was beginning. In the ring, which was lined with crowds of people, the huge beasts were being lined up and judged by a woman in a traditional black and white striped referee shirt. The judge walked up and down the line, feeling muscles, inspecting teeth, much like an AKC show, except these dogs weren't exactly the well-trained creatures one saw there. They were being forced to sit and stay and looked like they'd rather be elsewhere.

There were about six men and one woman competing and in the end, a solid brown bully took the prize. I think it was for best female, because each dog sported huge nipples, clearly indicating the life of a breeder.

I'd had had enough. As I headed out, I stopped at the rescue booth again to say goodbye to Michelle and to meet the other two organizations who shared the space.

One was ResQ Awearness, which produced a line of very cool graphic style T-shirts in the vein of Affliction and Sinful. A portion of their sales benefit rescue groups. The second was Heaven Sent Pit Bull, a non-profit which rescues, rehabilitates, and trains pit bulls to become AKC Canine Good Citizens and therapy dogs. Eventually, some become service dogs that are placed with the physically or mentally challenged. Sherise Davila, a single mom of three, ran the operation with the help of her children, including Hunter, who had sold me a $20 T-shirt after his impassioned plea.

Since I hit it off right away ResQ Awearness co-owner Kathleen Mannix and her son Jake Bunn, I asked them to dinner. I always enjoy hanging out with rescue people and told them to invite Michelle and her husband as well as Sherise and her kids.

It was about 2 p.m. and I needed to pick up Loren. She came out from the groomer with a bright multi-colored girly ribbon around her collar and a happy expression. I kissed her on top of her fresh-smelling head and she reciprocated with a long lick on my nose.

That's one thing I never saw at the show. People being affectionate with their dogs. Why would they, though? They were clearly accessories, status symbols, like sports cars or expensive shoes. They were not pets or companion animals. I marveled that Loren, who has not had the easiest life, actually had it better than a lot of dogs.

We met at Crumpets for dinner, which had a lovely outdoor patio and a heavily vegetarian menu, which I needed after all the barbecue and Mexican food I'd consumed. The weather was perfect for al fresco dining. I wore the free ResQ Awearness t-shirt Kathleen had given me. It was black, with an image of a dog who looked a lot like Loren amidst intricate designs and the word "aware-ness." Kathleen and her sister had created the company just three weeks before, looking for a creative way to improve the pit bull image while helping rescues. I loved it.

Kathleen and I ordered the vegetarian plate, which had grilled vegeta-bles, pasta with sundried tomatoes and pine nuts and best of all, melted brie on crunchy, toasted bread. If there's anything better than melted cheese and fresh, toasty bread, I have yet to find it.

Sherise and Hunter joined us as we were deciding on dessert. Hunter quickly took Loren's leash and asked if he could walk her. Though he was only in fourth grade, this was one strong, pit bull savvy kid. He calmly led Loren through the lush, grassy yards surrounding the property.

His mother was in a quandary. The breeders at the show had gotten together for a raffle to donate money to her organization, but Sherise didn't know that they were raffling off a puppy. She felt guilty about taking the money, doing so only after meeting the family that had won and insisting on providing them with six months of free training.

"They seemed like a nice family," she said. "And they really wanted a dog, but didn't have the money for one."

We assured her she did the right thing and Sherise seemed to relax a little. In her low, husky voice, reminiscent of Alicia Keys, she told us she received about 100 calls a day, mostly from people trying to get rid of their pit bulls rather than wanting to adopt or get training. Sherise did what she could on limited funds and a busy schedule. All of the pits at Heaven Sent lived in the house with Sherise and her kids.

Hunter came back with Loren, who promptly tried to jump on Sherise's lap and smothered her with kisses. Sherrie held Loren close and smiled, obviously right at home, while Hunter asked if he could show us a picture. It was a shot of him, covered by a sleeping bag, surrounded by about ten bullies of various colors and sizes, all asleep together on the floor. It was beautiful.

"You never see photos like this on the news, but you'll sure see something about the event today," Sherise said. "Or dog fights. We have about three dog fighting rings a week broken up in San Antonio."

"Really?" I asked. "That's horrifying."

Sherise nodded. "Yes. That's why I bring my dogs to libraries, parks, schools, even the city council office, whenever I can. We have to turn the image around for these dogs, show that they aren't just gang dogs or fighting dogs."

When I suggested putting together a positive pet fair, showcasing pit bulls doing things like agility and providing adoptions to the public, Sherise looked at me wryly.

"Whoa, whoa, you keep saying adoption, but there aren't any pit bull rescues here besides me," she said.

"What about the shelters? Wouldn't they want to participate?" I asked.

Again, the cynical grin. "They don't adopt out pits in San Antonio. Shelters make them rescue only and there aren't any rescues stepping up, so they get killed," she said. "They're trying to ban them. San Antonio is not pit bull friendly."

Wow. Every time I thought I saw progress for pit bulls, I heard something like this and it stopped me in my tracks. I had to give it to the ABKC breeders. They had found the one way to get around BSL, by creating a sanctioned breed. Instead of saving the dogs that already existed, they just bypassed the issue by introducing more dogs into the world while millions died in shelters. It defied logic, at least mine.

All of us were exhausted from the long, crazy day and headed to our respective cars, lingering in the parking lot as we continued to talk. Typical rescuers. As I said my goodbyes, I confessed that my biggest fear while traveling was seeing a stray pit bull or a chained pit bull.

Sherise shot me a look, eyebrows furrowed, sadness filling her dark brown eyes.

"I wish that was the worst thing that we saw," she said. "We get calls on dead dogs. From fighting or neglect."

Kathleen and I were temporarily shocked into silence as Sherise continued. "We bury them," she said, her dark brown eyes turning liquid. "We try to give them a little peace and show them some love."

The Big Easy

You know you're in Louisiana when billboards start announcing things like "Gator Country!" and "Got Hurricane Claims?" I was just happy to get the hell out of Texas and into a new state.

Around 11:30, lunch was calling my name. I used Gidget to find a Cajun or Creole place in Lafayette and was directed to the Creole Café. Since the vibe reminded me too much of Yo Momma, I looked in my *Roadfood* book and went to Prejean's instead. We pulled off the freeway and drove back up alongside it for a mile or so. I was thrilled their entrance sign announced that the restaurant had

"Can't pose now, I'm on gator watch!"

shaded kennels for dogs while diners enjoyed their meals. How cool is that?

Not cool enough for Loren. The kennels were kind of small, more appropriate for a Maltese or maybe a Sheltie, not my long, lanky Loren, so I left her in the truck under a large shade tree, watched over by their handyman named Marco. She must have liked it alright, because the alarm didn't go off once.

Inside Prejean's, a huge cavern-like restaurant with three rooms, it was pure Cajun camp, with stuffed gators galore and a live Zydeco band. While I have an adventurous palate, I bypassed the alligator dishes and ordered a cup of the chicken and sausage gumbo and an ala carte crawfish enchilada. The gumbo was rich, yet smoky and spicy, chock full of chicken and andouille sausage, while the enchilada was a medley of cream, Cajun spices, and tender crawfish. My dreams of eating in Louisiana were not only coming true, but surpassing my expectations.

I told my waiter Matthew so and that this was my first stop in Louisiana. "You picked a good place to start," he replied.

We got to talking. Matthew had a pit bull once, which he re-homed when his homeowner's insurance company informed him it wouldn't cover the dog for liability.

"There are plenty of insurance providers that don't exclude breeds like pit bulls. Farmer's and State Farm among them, I believe," I told Matthew.

"Well, if I ever adopt one again, and I want to, I'll make sure I'm ready," Matthew said. I handed him a postcard.

On the way out, I picked up a homemade Prejean's praline, a 6-inch hard disc of butter, brown sugar, cream, and nuts. I opened it in the car and took a nibble. Sweet, yet slightly savory from the butter and nuts, rich and creamy, it momentarily made me forget all about chocolate, my go-to sweet. I ate about half of the praline on the way to New Orleans, a two-hour drive.

Loren looked at me as if to say, "Where's mine?"

"Sorry girl," I said, patting her on the head. "Some things are not meant for puppies."

She jumped in the back and, with a heavy sigh, began to nap as we crossed a freeway that spanned miles over swampland. Muddy, dark green water, covered in algae, was just yards underneath our car, an experience I'd never had driving before. I wondered how many bodies had been dumped over the side of the highway to disappear forever without a trace. "Born on the Bayou," with its thick, murky bass line and spooky guitar licks, began to play in my head. Like placing a name to a face, the landscape put a place to a song I've always loved.

The skies were overcast, which turned into full blown rain, with huge drops splotching on the windshield. Thoughts of Hurricane Katrina naturally followed. I felt like we were driving through history as we approached the downtown area, including the infamous Superdome where people were evacuated during the storm. Inside that huge gray concrete dome, incredibly sad and surreal situations festered. I couldn't imagine being stuck in a large, stifling hot building with thousands of strangers who just lost everything and had nowhere else to go. It must have been horrible.

Our hotel was about a half mile from the French Quarter, which was a bit seedier than I expected. Rathbone Mansion was an elegant, 10-room white three-story home built in 1846 with black wrought iron accents and a huge brick porch. The neighborhood was a melange of narrow, brightly colored houses and new luxury apartments, as well as some hurricane-damaged homes that were vacated and spray painted with a huge black X.

We were given a first level room and I loved the black and white art deco accents, big bed with fluffy comforter, and hardwood floors. Better yet, we were the only human/canine duo checked in for the duration of our stay, so Loren had the run of the long driveway, which was gated off from the streets.

"Come on girl," I said, slapping my thighs and running to and from the fence. She jumped back, then forward, making a mad, wild dash toward me and taking off for the 100 or so yard stretch like an Olympic sprinter. I giggled in disbelief and amusement. Loren did a few laps, then stopped, a big silly grin on her face, her eyes sparkling. Usually so dignified, it was a treat to see her let loose.

Reluctantly this time, Loren jumped in the truck and we drove down to Decatur Street so I could pick up a muffuletta sandwich from Central Grocery, one of the culinary things to do in New Orleans. Somehow, on a busy day, we snagged a decent parking spot right on the main street. I bid Loren a short adieu and walked up the road, holding my camera around my neck, trying to affect a somewhat tough stance. Most people just ignored me, caught up in their own drama.

A junkie slept against his crutches in the street. Grizzled men shot the breeze on stools outside their favorite bars, which are so steeped with the stench of beer and cigarettes, it wafted outside to the street. Foodies were lined up at their favorite restaurants. Carriage drivers made their rounds. Tourists shopped for quirky trinkets, such as Absinthe spoons advertised outside one store.

Unfortunately, Central Grocery, world-renowned for their muffulettas, a New Orleans-borne creation of Italian cold cuts and cheese lavished with homemade olive salad, were sold out of the sandwiches. Disappointed, I went to Frank's a few doors down, to get their version to go. I was worried about Loren in the car by herself, even with a lock and alarm system. There were some shady characters lingering about.

Briskly making my way back to the truck, I saw two men on the street, one tapping a brown substance from a plastic bag into a folding paper. My eyes grew wide, but I didn't miss a beat.

We went back to the hotel, where I fed Loren and ate half of my half - sandwich, which was good - soft bread, fresh cold cuts, rich cheese, piquant olives - but not incredible, especially for the $9 I paid. To take our second to last potty break of the night, we headed across the street from the hotel, where there was a big grassy field.

A man, probably in his late 50s, was walking his elderly black and white Border Collie, which reminded me of my beloved Willy, the sweetest member of my pack who had died about five years before. We smiled and waved at one another in what I thought was an act of dog lover camaraderie.

A few minutes later, about 100 feet away, the man took off his head-phones and yelled over. "Hey sweetie. Great butt!"

I was shocked. At first, I thought, me or Loren? I was wearing big old baggy khaki capris for Christ's sake and hadn't even taken a shower. I shook my head in disbelief and walked quickly in the opposite direction. Maybe he thought it was a compliment. I just thought it was creepy.

Like Houston, New Orleans freaked me out a bit. I came to the realiza-tion that I'm just not real comfortable in big cities. The hallmark of my suburban childhood, I suppose. I vowed to overcome it and enjoy what this city had to offer, but honestly, I was a little scared.

With the night winding down, Loren was happy to snooze on the bed, which I dubbed Mission Control, since there wasn't a desk. Her feet touching mine, Loren would peek at me occasionally as I updated our blog from the laptop, appropriately placed on my lap, taking frequent breaks to reach over and rub her belly.

Lonely, slightly hormonal and missing my boyfriend, friends, and peaceful mountain home, I was tripped out about our trip. I wondered what the hell I was thinking to do this. At other times, I felt so lucky and alive and engaged at the opportunity to see this incredible country I live in. It was just hard sometimes not to let the minutiae or fear get in the way. Outside our homey room was a strange, sometimes dangerous city, and we didn't know a soul in it.

***

Getting into the slower-paced Southern vibe, Loren and I slept in. I'd come up with several new nicknames for her. "Come on, Loren Bacall," I would say, patting her butt as she stretched in the morning. "Let's get a move on, Sophia Loren." I also began calling her Boogie T. Boo and Booger for short.

The area and our hotel were becoming home quickly. People here really seemed to be a community. They hung out on their porches and barbequed, drank, or just chatted. It was hard not to feel a part of it. There were a lot of dog walkers, too, which unlike the pervert from the day before, would congenially wave and smile without further comment.

Thankfully, no stray dogs approached us. We did see a golden shepherd/retriever mix roaming around the day before, from the safety of our truck, but he seemed to be heading somewhere, so I prayed it was a case of a canine cruise through the neighborhood rather than one of homelessness.

There was a recovery meeting at a coffee shop a few miles away. It took some time finding, as the streets are endless and usually one way, so if you missed a turn, it was a loop until you could get back on course. Though unintentional, getting a little off track gave me an opportunity to see some of the extreme poverty here, how slow the rebuilding efforts were, that many people in this country really do without a lot of the things I take for granted. New Orleans and what Hurricane Katrina had wrought went from an impersonal news story to a reality for me.

During the meeting, I shared about our trip, and afterward, while waiting for a lemon mango iced tea at the coffeehouse below, I felt a tap on my shoulder.

"Hey," a 20-something guy dressed in shorts and T-shirt said to me. "Do you know who Ken Foster is?"

"Yes," I said, surprised that this guy did. Ken Foster is the author of *Dogs That Have Found Me*, a great book I devoured on vacation in Homer, Alaska, attracted by the cover photo of a black and white pit bull.

"He lives here. You should Google him and drop him an email. I've heard he's really cool and would probably meet you, if he has the time," he said.

"Wow, that's cool. Thanks," I said.

The guy smiled at me and walked away. "Good luck," he said over his shoulder.

After the meeting, we came back to our room and as Loren settled in for a snooze, I couldn't resist. After I found Ken Foster's email address and introduced myself, I snuggled next to Loren and took a nap in air-conditioned comfort, getting up around 1 p.m. to go for lunch.

The French Quarter was particularly lively that day, as it was Memorial Day weekend. I scoped out a restaurant, using shade and the ability to keep an eye on my girl in the truck as the main criteria. Oceana had a picture window seat facing the street and it was on the shady side. Down the road, a live band was wailing out *Bobby McGee* with conviction. Not even nearing darkness, the city was already a party.

I went tourist and ordered "A Taste of New Orleans," a combo plate of jambalaya, red beans, rice, sausage, and crawfish etoufee. The latter was the best, though my good friend Michelle Vincent makes a much better version. I'm not much of a jambalaya person, I've discovered; it tastes too much like marinara sauce, which never floated my boat. The red beans and rice were delish, though, smoky and rich, and the sausage was excellent (you can never go wrong with sausage). The waiter was nice, too, supplying me with an endless stream of Arnold Palmers.

Loren and I hit the streets briefly afterwards for a walk and people-watching. She was a big hit wherever we went.

"Wow, she's beautiful," I heard three times.

"Wow, she's really built," was another common theme.

Loren just kept her nose on the concrete trail, excited when she discovered a mysterious cloudy liquid. Before I knew it, she flipped on her back and was rolling around in it.

"Loren, that's gross. Get up," I said, pulling her leash sharply.

She grinned like a mischievous kid. Sometimes I forgot Loren was a dog…and that dogs can sometimes be disgusting.

"She must have found some dead bodies," someone cracked as they walked by.

No, but Loren did find some chicken bones on the floor of a daiquiri bar I made an ill-decided shortcut through. These were like Icees for adults, a dozen colorful flavors swirling around and waiting to be dispensed. I pulled her quickly out of there; not exactly the best place for either of us. Loren hacked up the bones on the sidewalk and we were on our way.

In the mood for some reading beyond my travel guides and local newspapers, I found the Fauborg Marigny Arts Books & Music Store at 600 Frenchman. This place is about as far from your neighborhood Barnes & Noble as you can get, with scattered subjects, prominently displayed gay porn, and flashy local characters mingling in and out.

The flamboyantly dressed owner was very helpful, leading me, ironically enough, straight to Ken Foster's *Dogs I Have Met*. I also selected *Me Talk Pretty One Day* by David Sedaris and *America Anonymous* by Benoit Denizet-Lewis, satisfied they would keep me occupied for quite some time.

But first, there was dinner to attend to. I took a shower to get ready for my big meal at Commander's Palace. I blew dry my hair instead of pinning it up in my usual haphazard bun for this special occasion, and traded my daily jeans and T-shirt uniform for black pants and a sleeveless tangerine cotton wraparound shirt. Loren and I stepped outside for a brief walk, but by the time we got back, boom, my hair had poofed up into a cloud around my head, like a bad 80s perm. For this reason alone, I could never live in the South.

The valets at the restaurant let me park in the front, where it was shady and they could keep an eye on Loren. I poured her a bowl of water, placed it on the truck's floor, then pursed my lips for a goodbye kiss, which she granted happily.

"She might set off the alarm," I warned as I handed them the keys.

"Don't worry about it," the young male valet responded. "Just have a good time."

It was a certain thrill going to Commander's Palace, which is located in the upscale garden district, where mansions are aplenty. I have seen this place on the Food Network and read about it a thousand times. As I was led to an upstairs table, I watched in awe as a corps of waiters simultaneously served a table of eight, lifting silver domes off of plates, as graceful as a synchronized swimming routine.

I ordered the three-course chef's dinner with shrimp & char chili soup, soft shell crab atop a bed of greens and blue crab, and pecan pie for dessert, as well as my favorite mocktail, a cranberry and club soda with lime. The soup was amazing - just the right amount of heat against the tender shrimp - and the crab even more so, crispy fried perfection, its creamy interior cut with an acidic tang from the tomatoes and vinaigrette. I was so full, I took the pecan pie back to the room.

Loren and I wandered outside before getting ready for bed. Our hotel was really growing on me. We had the courtyard practically to ourselves and lounged by the pool for a while. The summer sky was muggy and overcast and Loren ran surveillance around the perimeter before settling on the lounge chair at my feet. Together, we watched the sun go down. It was a damn fine Sunday evening.

***

Having been told a trip to Café Du Monde for beignets and café au lait was required while staying in The Big Easy, that was our initial morning destination. As we waited at a red light, a woman, looking intently at our magnets, walked over and asked me if I had a card. I handed her a postcard and she briefly pet Loren.

"He was homeless before we rescued him," she said, nodding at her fluffy, rust-colored dog.

"That's awesome," I said with a big grin. "Bless you for rescuing."

The light turned green and we waved goodbye.

At Café Du Monde, the scene was much quieter than the 50 to 100 deep line I had witnessed the afternoon before. There were only a few people waiting, though it still took a long time to place my order. Things are not super efficient in New Orleans but it was a nice change from the often hyper-rushed pace of Southern California.

Four dollars later, I had my beignets and coffee. The small doughnut-like pastries were a bit greasy and doused in powdered sugar. There was an inch of powder at the bottom of the paper bag and about a half-ton spilled on the floor in the small dining room. The coffee was a little bitter for my palate. All in all, not the must-experience taste sensation I'd anticipated.

Since the morning cooled way down and rain started to pour, we went back to our room instead of exploring the area more. It was a serendipitous move, as I'd received a return email from Ken Foster. He agreed to meet me and Loren for lunch. I was surprised and a little nervous. Ken was a real, published author and I was just some crazy reporter/blogger, but we had the dogs in common.

We originally scheduled to meet at Willie Mae's Scotch Kitchen, which the Food Network hailed as having the best fried chicken in America, but they were not open for business that day. The Praline Connection was our backup plan and it was a pleasant surprise. Crisp white linen were on both the tables and the servers, who also donned snappy black hats.

The chicken was great, as Ken had assured me it would be; crisp, succulent, slightly spicy. He often stopped here on the way back from his local teaching gig.

Of course, we mostly talked dogs. Ken has four now, two males and two females, which started with Sula, his beautiful pit bull featured on "Dogs Who Found Me." He named his non-profit organization after her, The Sula Foundation, which has an active foster network and regularly holds educational/fundraising events in New Orleans to fund their rescue efforts.

I told Ken about the curious reaction I was getting from people when I walked Loren, especially from some tough-looking characters I thought would never be afraid of her. These people actually crossed the street as we approached them, which I found amusing. If they only knew. Loren and I were harmless, the marshmallow twins.

"You have to remember, people from these neighborhoods usually know pit bulls one of two ways - either through dog fighting or as a drug dealer's enforcement," he said.

Like Los Angeles, the New Orleans shelter system is overrun with pit bulls, many from backyard breeders who think they can make a quick buck.

"I ask them how much they think they'll get for a puppy and they say, $1,000," Ken said incredulously.

I laughed. "Really? Are they on crack?"

Maybe not, but a lot of them probably sell it, along with pit bull puppies. These unscrupulous breeders are lucky to get $100 for their puppies. Most of the dogs end up in the shelter, like a little white, deaf girl whom Ken was boarding at the Animal Clinic on Magazine Street. One of 13 pups, her breeder immediately took the dog to the shelter when he realized she was deaf, refusing to pay the $10 owner surrender fee. He drove off in a shiny new SUV.

We went to pick up some puppy food at the Canine Connection on Magazine Street, a really clean and colorful doggy day care and boarding facility. Their canine greeter, Wendy, a shepherd mix of a certain age, had been rescued by the shop owner from the shelter, where she was scheduled for euthanasia for being too old and unadoptable. Wendy looked about seven or eight and was certainly spry enough to come over to every visitor and lean against their legs until she was pet. They were also boarding an adorable little black terrier mix who had been rescued from a neglect situation.

Since the vet wouldn't be open until 2 p.m., Ken and I took Loren for a walk. She took a shine to him instantly, showering Ken with kisses and minding him quite well, though she insisted on poking her head into almost every store and bar we came across, trying to introduce herself. Sure enough, the hardcore guys with beanie caps and baggie jeans avoided Loren at all costs, moving from the sidewalk into the street as we passed one another.

Once we returned to the animal clinic, Loren settled back into the truck so I could meet the puppy, a cutie with one blue eye and one green eye. Is there anything more adorable than a puppy, especially a white pit bull puppy? She ran to and from everyone, a little white blur, still awkward like a foal, making us all laugh.

We tossed around potential names for her, with my clever mind coming up with Scampi (because she likes to scamper about) and Praline.

"Ugh," Ken said of the latter. "I don't like anything that sounds too New Orleans."

Antoine, the vet, was very loving toward the little puppy as she ran to and fro, taking an especially keen interest in the bags of dog food near the floor. He told us of a local man who crops pit bull ears and dispenses fake medications and vaccinations. All with no license, of course.

"I must have to clean up his mess at least once a month," he sighed. "I'm getting tired of it."

***

Antoine isn't the only one tired of the mistreatment pit bulls and other dogs in his city suffer. The staff and volunteers at Animal Rescue New Orleans, a no-kill shelter in Jefferson, work tirelessly to rescue stray dogs and cats found starving and injured on the city's sometimes harsh streets.

Located in an industrial area, ARNO, as it is known, occupies a small warehouse full of crates, kennels, and runs, sheltering both dogs and cats. The all-volunteer rescue sprang up after Hurricane Katrina and has since placed more than 6,000 animals in their forever homes.

"Is that good?" Charlotte Bass Lilly asked me as we barreled along in her Mercedes station wagon toward our dining destination uptown. Charlotte, the executive director of ARNO, had agreed to meet me for dinner after an email introduction via Traci Donellan Howerton, whom I met on the rescue's Facebook page. Loren was resting comfortably, I hoped, in a spacious ARNO outdoor kennel.

"That's amazing," I told her. "The Brittany Foundation, where I volunteer, has placed about 1,400 dogs since it started in 1993."

"Oh, that makes me feel better," she said. "Sometimes I don't feel as if that's a high enough number."

Though petite in height, Charlotte immediately commanded attention, with her olive skin, thick brunette hair jauntily piled on top of her head and cool black-rimmed glasses. She had a husky voice and laughed easily. I would have pegged her for a New Yorker, if not for the faint Southern drawl.

Charlotte had hugged me when I first stuck out my hand and moved piles of towels, treats, and other assorted donations from her passenger seat in order to make room for me.

"What can I say? It's a rescuer car," she said and I giggled in recognition.

"I get it. You should see my truck," I said.

"I drive fast, too," she said, taking the corner of the winding street like a racetrack driver.

"That's cool, I do too," I replied.

I liked Charlotte already.

Traci was waiting for us at Cafe Atchafalaya, a young Crystal Gayle with long, shiny black hair, wide blue eyes and a charming Southern accent. There was live contemporary music, black clad waiters, white linen topped tables, and an incredible menu featuring fresh local seafood. My dining companions ordered drinks and I a cranberry and club soda with lime.

We decided to share a long line of appetizers, starting with fried oysters, tender underneath their shatteringly crisp cornmeal breading and decadent, spicy sauce.

"You have to eat the whole thing at once," Charlotte instructed. "There's the oyster and its belly and they need to be eaten together to get the full effect."

I did so and rolled my eyes heavenward in satisfaction as the tender taste of the sea exploded in my mouth.

"That is so good," I said. "That is incredible."

The fried green tomatoes, crunchy, perfectly fried discs of earthy succulence underneath a blanket of peppery cream sauce, were another revelation. Even the salads here are thoughtfully and creatively composed; we ordered the fresh greens dressed in a light vinaigrette with sweet and savory candied pecans, shaved slices of pear, and pungent blue cheese.

Next came the freeform ravioli, stuffed with fresh, sweet lump crabmeat, sautéed shiitake mushrooms and spinach, finished with a lemon butter sauce. Charlotte also let me have a bite of her crab cake, which was nearly all sweet lump meat under its butter-rich crumb coating and creamy remoulade sauce.

"Oh my god," I said. "Everything's incredible. I love Cajun food."

"Honey, when you're in New Orleans, it's Creole food, not Cajun," Charlotte explained gently. "Anyway, eating is a sport here. Everyone's got their favorite dishes and restaurants and you can get into some pretty heated debates about it."

Since all of us had a background in marketing and public relations, conversation was easy, whether we talked about work, dogs, or family. Traci, a

Louisiana native, had been married at a church down the street shortly following Hurricane Katrina. She and her husband had temporarily evacuated to California, but came back to the state Traci knew and loved to start their new life together.

"We figured if we could make it through the cross country travel and living with relatives and all the chaos, that anything else that would come our way should be easy," she said.

It's impossible not to think of the hurricane when in New Orleans. It's left an indelible mark, not just on property, but on its residents souls. On the ride back, Charlotte told me stories about Katrina that made my hair curl quicker than the heavy Southern humidity.

She was a volunteer at Lamar Dixon animal shelter at the time and said there were thousands of displaced animals crowded under one roof. The temporary volunteers, though kind-hearted, didn't know what to do with them all. They would cut off old collars, to Charlotte's amazement.

"'What are you doing?' I would ask them. 'Don't you know that could be the only form of identification linking a pet to its owner? Their only connection?'" she rolled her eyes, taking a hit off her cigarette, politely holding it next to the open window so the smoke avoided me.

Charlotte revealed she has a bad back that requires surgery, but was too scared to go under the knife. "Funny, though, during the storm, I was throwing 70 pound pit bulls over my back and it didn't hurt," she said.

A few weeks after the hurricane, a friend had asked Charlotte to check on her dogs and cats as she'd had to leave them behind during an evacuation. Two dogs and many, many cats. Charlotte told her friend that she didn't hold out much hope for the dogs, but reassured her that the cats were probably OK.

"She had high beams in her house, in the attic," Charlotte said. "Sure enough, all her cats were perched up there. The dogs, though, they didn't make it. It was really sad, because you could see paw prints above where the water had risen."

She looked at me, brown eyes glistening. I shook my head in disbelief. "The worst thing was when you would find a dead body," Charlotte said.

"Human?" I asked tentatively.

"Oh yeah. If you found one you were supposed to tie it to a tree or some place stationary so rescue crews could locate it," she replied, blowing out a stream of smoke. "We called Katrina the great equalizer. White, black, young, old, everyone looks the same after you've been in the water for a few weeks."

***

Like most rescues, ARNO was a hubbub of activity in the morning. Dogs know they are going to be fed and walked and loved on by volunteers and they can't wait. According to Charlotte, volunteers come from all over the country and even the world to help out at their facility.

It was 9 a.m., and after reading the volunteer protocol about cleaning, feeding and walking and signing a release, I was ready to go. Loren was placed in the 10' x 10' outdoor kennel she had occupied the night before, with a big fan blowing on her. Her neighbors were Kaia, a sweet young golden mixed breed who didn't like other dogs, and Bear, a massive older black lab mix who didn't like people messing with his territory, aka his kennel, which he lounged around in like a king, splayed out on his big comfy dog bed.

ARNO has several sections. The hallway leading up to the lobby/kitchen area is lined with cat cages, approximately 50, with felines of all ages and sizes and colors, some with special needs, clearly indicated by brightly colored signs. A woman from Colorado was cleaning out litter boxes and handling the feedings. She comes five times a year, one week at a time, to do so. The cats were mellow, taking naps on their little hammocks or snuggled deep into their circular beds.

Inside the dog kennels, things were a bit more hectic. The morning routine involved one volunteer, who took a dog out for a 10-15 minute walk, carrying poop bags to clean up any messes along the way. This allowed another volunteer time to clean the kennel or crate with Trifectant, followed by water, and finally, preparing his or her daily meal, a combination of kibble moistened with a few tablespoons of wet food for flavor. With breakfast waiting, the dogs were pretty happy to return.

Grateful, a brown and white pit bull with cropped ears that looked a bit like Loren, was my first walk of the day. She was raring to go, so off we went, down the street and across the railroad tracks, until we hit a large, grassy patch. Grateful immediately launched herself onto her back and wiggled across the grass, back and forth, scratching herself and rolling over multiple times. She was exalted.

It was times like this that I truly appreciated dogs. Who knew what had happened to this poor girl, living in a crate now, awaiting a new home? In the meantime, she was going to make the best of the present and for now, that meant splendor in the grass.

After a few more walks, it was my turn to clean kennels. I watched as Lily was tenderly carried from her crate to the sidewalk by a volunteer.

"That's a French bulldog, right?" I asked Jeff Benskin, the head volunteer who lives on the premises. Tall, in his 40s with strawberry blonde hair and tanned, freckled skin from the hard outdoor work he performs each day, Jeff had come to ARNO to help out after Hurricane Gustav, planning on staying for one day. Two years later, he's still there.

"Actually, she's a Boston Terrier," he said.

"She sure is cute. She'll get snapped up right away, don't you think?" I asked.

"You would think so. But she's been here for a few months," Jeff replied.

I sighed. "There's no rhyme or reason to this, is there?" I asked.

"No, there really isn't," he said.

How could this cute young purebred dog end up a shelter for months? It was crazy. I've never understood why some dogs get adopted and others remain for months, even years. At The Brittany Foundation, I watched in astonishment as Frankie, a grumpy, yappy 11-year old Yorkie got snapped up almost immediately by a family while eight-year old Miley Cyrus, an adorable Yorkie with wombat ears and the sweetest personality, stayed behind for another year until a foster family finally took her in.

After cleaning, it was playtime in the side yard, a long concrete fenced-in area where ARNO dogs got to frolic, city style. Victoria Clark, a 16 year-old volunteer who resembled a teenage Christina Ricci, was a girl of few words but in obvious command of her surroundings, showing us volunteers how to wrangle shepherd mixes Jackson, Carrollton and their five lively pups from their large kennel into the yard.

Carrollton was named for being found on Carrollton Street. She had a broken leg and was lactating, which led the ARNO crew to search for her puppies located just a few blocks away. Carrollton's owner reluctantly signed the puppies over to ARNO (he was fine to get rid of mama, though) and now three of the remaining five were in process of being adopted. Puppies tend to go quick.

Once in the play yard, the little black and tan furballs scampered about, making toys out of whatever they could find, plastic bottles and strips of cloth, playing tug of war and jumping in and out of the pool as their frazzled parents watched on.

"Jackson's just their stepdad," Victoria explained in a low voice. "He was already here and they liked each other, so he's part of the family now."

"Yeah," Jeff said. "She didn't tell them until after the first date that she had five kids. Typical woman."

We all laughed. Inside the play yard was Derek, a local teenager who originally started volunteering as a way to placate his family for being expelled from school, but who was now warming up to the animals, and Margaret, a retiree from Wisconsin who comes down twice a year to volunteer.

Maverick was next up for a walk. The big, black pit mix was an extreme example of the Loren school of walking: start, stop, act stubborn, and repeat. Except Maverick really didn't want to move at all, no matter how hard I tried to coerce him. Victoria suggested I take him in the yard and play fetch.

Suddenly, this reticent dog came to life, running for the ball and bringing it back before gently dropping it either behind the forklift or near my feet, depending on his mood. He moved kind of slowly, at least compared to most pits I knew.

"How old is he?" I asked Jeff, who was cleaning out water bowls near the fence.

"Not that old, believe it or not," he said.

I checked Maverick's teeth, which is a good way to gauge a dog's age, and was horrified to see his canines ground down to flat little nubs.

"Wow," I said to Jeff. "He was a bait dog, wasn't he?" Bait dogs are used to entice fighting dogs to, well, fight. Most don't make it out of that scenario alive.

"Probably," Jeff said sadly. "We don't know for sure."

I threw the ball and watched Maverick retrieve it with gusto.

"You know what's sad?" I said to Jeff. "In another life, under different circumstances, Maverick would be someone's perfect backyard dog, happy to play catch and run around with the kids."

"I know what you mean," he said.

My stomach was sending me hunger signals. It was 1 p.m. Time for lunch. I bid Maverick adieu and drove a few blocks, coming across T-Bobs, a slightly shady-looking joint that advertised hot lunches. For some reason, no matter how scorching it is outside (and it was pretty warm that day) I still enjoy eating a hot meal. You'll rarely if ever see me eating a salad as an entree.

I ordered the shrimp po boy and it was overstuffed with crispy little fried nuggets. Impatient, I gulped it down it too soon and burned the roof of my mouth. It was my second injury of the day. I had acquired a large blood blister on my finger earlier that morning from misjudging the kennel gate latch. I am not known for my grace or coordination.

It was now 1:30 and an entirely different scene in the kennels when I returned. All I could hear were the immense fans blowing. The dogs were laying on their sides, like overgrown cats. It reminded me of The Brittany Foundation, after everyone had their walks or recess in the dog run. It was nap time.

It was a very touching sight. Though it's not as ideal as a home, at least they were being taken care of here at ARNO. For many, it's a vast improvement from their life on the street or on the end of a chain or being tied up in a basement with just a cardboard box to do its business in, as was the case for Arby, a rather spastic Cocker Spaniel that I took for an afternoon walk. Brenna, a small bully mix, had rough, black skin and sparse fur from an extreme case of mange and the reddest eyes I'd ever seen, a result, I was told, from being kicked in the head. She was probably quite happy to be at ARNO.

Little Red immediately stole my heart. She was a condensed, darker caramel version of Loren, but just as sweet, with low-hanging nipples from her past as a breeder. Little Red was in an isolation room next to the cats, getting treated for heartworm, and thrilled to get out for a few minutes. Once on the lawn, she leapt onto her back for impromptu scratching, which elicited belly rubs and smiles from me. Pit bulls. Such shameless hussies and clowns.

"I love her," I told Jeff as we approached the entrance. "She reminds me a lot of Loren."

"That's what I thought," Jeff said. "Everyone else said that Grateful was Loren's twin, but I thought she was more like Little Red."

As I washed up and got ready to leave, I joined Victoria briefly in the cat room. She was gently cradling Buzz Lightyear, a two and a half week old kitten, just having bottle fed him. He was the runt of the litter and, Victoria calmly informed me, had just a 50/50 chance of making it.

"I need to find someone to take care of him when I get back to school," she said. "Maybe my school counselor will keep him in her office and let me feed him during my breaks."

According to Victoria, she's the only animal lover in her family. She spends every free moment at ARNO: spring break, summer, holidays and weekends. Victoria, who's been volunteering at ARNO since she was 12, told me that she wants to be a veterinarian, a marine biologist or a professional clarinet player.

"If I'm not able to volunteer anymore, I'll come back to ARNO and adopt the ones that don't find homes because they're dog aggressive or whatever," she said in her shy, but assertive way.

I said goodbye to Victoria and headed to the restroom for one last pit stop, then

"Victoria, I am putty in your hands!"

53

through the maze of runs and crates to pick up Loren. To my surprise, Victoria was inside the kennel with her, sitting on the ground, hugging Loren tight. Loren was lapping it up. They looked very cozy.

"She's special," Victoria said.

"She is, huh? Of course, I think so, but then I wonder if I am biased," I responded.

"No, she's really different. She's an awesome dog," Victoria said, lighting up in Loren's presence, a faint smile on her usually somber face.

"Yeah, I know. I just don't get why she hasn't found a family yet," I said.

"Some dogs just take longer than others, but they eventually find the right person. Loren will find hers," Victoria said, looking beneath her heavy dark bangs and into my eyes.

Somehow her quiet conviction reassured me.

Southern Belles

The lush highways to Alabama were a breeze to navigate, only 133 straight miles, which was a jaunt compared to the 350 to 400 mile stretches through Arizona and Texas. Like a trip to the grocery store

We checked into our free motel in Mobile and were happy to see the faux bamboo floors and subdued linens, giving the place a retro feel rather than a hyper-tropical one. They even had some fruit, crackers, and water waiting for us.

Loren was really excited most of the afternoon. There were about a half dozen kids playing around the pool and she watched them through the window, her ears perking up as they screamed and played. As usual, she wanted to be part of the scene, but I had errands to attend to.

That didn't mean we couldn't take a little fun break of our own. I grabbed Loren's stuffed toy that Nancy had packed, a little blue cat, and waved it in front of her face. She cocked her head and looked at the toy, then to me.

"Wanna play, Boogie?" I asked, then threw the cat. "Get the woobie!"

To my surprise, Loren sprang into action, her nails sliding on the slippery floor as she screeched to a halt, almost banging into the bathroom cabinet. She grabbed the woobie and shook it in a frenzy, then jumped on the bed and thrashed it about some more. I began to laugh.

Loren jumped off the bed again and tossed the woobie high into the air. It landed near the door and she slid across the floor to retrieve it before attacking the bed again, the bedspread beginning to resemble an afternoon romp of another kind. She repeated the maneuver a few more times and the laughter rumbled through my chest, the rich, beautiful kind that seems to relax every fiber of your being.

Finally, Loren dropped the woobie on the bed, her tongue hanging out, with a smug, satisfied expression. I sat beside her and stroked her back. "You're too much, Booger," I said fondly. She laid on her side and lifted her arm for a belly rub.

"I am the woobie master!"

There was laundry to do, so I loaded up a bag with dirty clothes and went off in search of the washers and dryers. That's when I saw two pit puppies in the parking lot, tied to a fence. Was this my worst fear coming true? When I came closer, I saw they both had tags and collars. Their mom, a pretty young brunette, came out and looked at me suspiciously.

"I hope you don't mind, I just wanted to make sure someone didn't dump them," I said.

She smiled.

"No, I don't mind, but we would never dump them. They are our babies," came the reply, tinged with a sweet Southern accent.

Angel told me she and her husband T.J. got their pit bulls, one who looked a lot like a baby Loren, from a breeder and had plans to breed them. My heart sank.

"Why would you breed pit bulls? There are so many in shelters who need homes," I said.

Angel raised a skeptical eyebrow.

"Where?" she asked. "Shelters won't adopt pit bulls out around here. I've checked."

I didn't know how to reply. Could that be true?

When I took Loren for a bathroom run, we met two maintenance men in the parking lot.

"Pretty dog," they exclaimed and rushed to pet her.

I told them about our trip and they revealed they were indirectly involved in rescue, too.

"I live at the end of a dirt road, so I don't need to look for animals. They find me when their owners dump them on my property," one of them said. "I have a Chihuahua, an Australian Shepherd and another purebred. All beautiful animals."

The other man substantiated Angel's claim about local shelters and pit bulls. "They won't adopt them out. They've had too many problems with fighting here," he said.

I had to find out the scoop for myself.

***

Mobile Animal Shelter is located off a main road in a woodsy area. It was mid-morning and Stacey Hamer, the shelter's animal resources supervisor, had agreed to be interviewed and explain the pit bull issue in Mobile firsthand. I pulled up and found a shady spot under a large leafy tree for Loren, giving her plenty of water and double checking that I locked the doors, paranoid she would somehow get out or be pulled from the truck by an animal control officer.

To the left of the shelter were several shaded chain-link outdoor dog runs with dozens of dogs, mostly puppies, scampering about. Really cute puppies: lab mixes, fluffy border collies, shepherds and terrier mixes in shades of white, gold, black, and brown.

Stacey met me in the lobby and assured me that Loren was safe in the car. Her clear blue eyes and dark brown hair were an arresting contrast and she had a shy, sweet smile. Stacey has been in rescue for more than 30 years and lives on a nearby seven-acre property called the Hallelujah Orphanage with her sister and a menagerie of animals: horses, dogs, cats, even an indoor/outdoor raccoon that shares a bed with her rescued pit bull.

With just three months of employment under her belt at the shelter, Stacey had already helped to almost triple their adoption rate, often by networking with rescues. She walked me around the kennels and gave me the story on each dog.

"That one's going to Long Dog Rescue. That one and her puppy are going to Lab Rescue. This one is being adopted on Saturday," she said, stopping at a cage where an older, mellow black lab female was sitting demurely. "This one's coming home with me. She gets overlooked a lot, but I love her personality."

The shelter takes in 30-40 animals per day and can accommodate up to 186, though the numbers can often swell to 200 or more. "Since this is puppy and kitten season, we can place four or five in a kennel," Stacey explained.

Their facility was built in 2009 and was pristinely clean, if a little austere, painted in shades of white, blue and grey. Kennels are about four feet wide by eight feet long, with shiny new stainless steel gates and a dog bed, toys, and treats placed in each. Dogs get out several times throughout the day to be socialized in the

Stacey Hamer, angel of Mobile Animal Shelter

outdoor kennels while the staff cleans, an efficient process thanks to the floor's state-of-the-art drainage system.

Border collies and lab mixes were the most predominant breeds. For some reason, Stacey said, border collies had a harder time being placed in the area, but she usually found spots in rescue for them at the last minute, when necessary.

I noted the kennel cards and was thrilled that Stacey really seemed to know her breeds and wasn't quick to label every other dog a pit bull mix. This is often the case at other shelters, where everything from boxers to bull dogs are categorized as pits, which can hasten their death sentence.

A black and brown beauty with blue eyes was noted as a bulldog mix, as was a gorgeous fawn and white new mama playing in the back with the general population. Stacey had confirmed that Mobile Animal Shelter doesn't adopt out pit bulls to the public (the same policy applies for wolf hybrids and chows over three months old).

"It's because of the population we're dealing with here in the South. There's a lot of dog fighting here," she explained. "There are people that come in and go straight to the pit bulls and say, 'I want that dog.' I'll ask why and they'll say because it's a pit. It goes back to protecting the animal. I can't tell you how many come in here scarred and injured. We know what they're used for."

Stacey works with groups like Bama Bully Rescue, a non-profit foster network throughout the state that places shelter pits with temporary families that ready them for adoption through socializing and housebreaking.

Otherwise, it's about a 95 percent euthanasia rate for pit bulls at the shelter, a statistic that breaks Stacey's heart.

"I have been in rescue for 30 years and I have never had a problem with a pit bull. I've never met a bad one. In fact, I find them to be devoted, extremely intelligent, fun dogs," she said. "I hate to see pits come in. The staff does, too. Our first comment is, that's a beautiful dog, too bad it's going down."

She described the process, which is performed by a certified euthanasia technician, as being as compassionate as possible under the circumstances, a lethal injection that takes just seconds to end an animal's life.

"Before an animal goes down, it is talked to and loved and given treats. They're not just thrown on the table. The people here care," Stacey said.

Tears stained my reporter's notebook as I struggled to take notes and when I looked up, Stacey's eyes met mine. They were glistening, as well.

"We are judged and called dog killers, but we're here because of what the public is doing. It's their responsibility," she said.

Following the procedure, bodies are stored in a freezer until they are taken to a landfill for disposal.

"I don't sleep at night," Stacey said. "I ask myself every day why I, an animal lover, am here. I can't stand the eyes of pain. But here, a lot of animals that would normally go down don't have to. God gives me the resources so they don't have to."

All the bully type breeds I met that day, Stacey assured me, were heading toward rescues, whether that meant in Alabama or via transport to out-of-state facilities. She often bought the dogs time beyond their seven day hold as strays or even shorter owner surrender periods by placing them in empty quarantine or observation kennels.

"Oh, I'm getting rescued? Thanks, Stacey!"

"Oh, we'll get them out of here," she said. "They don't come in and go down on the same day unless they are sick or aggressive."

Pregnant bullies hold an extra special place in Stacey's heart. She is currently fostering one herself. "These are the ones we have to make extra efforts for, so I really push our volunteers and fosters. I can't let mamas go down," Stacey said.

Because finances are so tight at the government funded facility, spay and neuter is not performed on outgoing animals, but rather is a requirement of the contract an adopter signs, to have their animal fixed within 30 days. Most people follow the rules, Stacey said, and her staff keeps earmarks on any adopters they even remotely suspect might be breeding with follow up phone calls and visits.

That lack of resources extends to the pit bull policy. As Stacey said, if the shelter had more volunteers or could recruit more rescues into providing their volunteers to perform home and background checks, she believes they could eventually make a real dent in the adoption of pit bulls in the area.

It's part of her ever-growing improvement list. The shelter is aligned with a group called Mobile Animal Rescue Community Outreach to try and improve the pit bull situation, as well as provide mobile spay and neuter clinics with local veterinarians and set up a pet food pantry for owners who have fallen on hard times.

Stacey is also currently working with local schools to provide humane education to students. "We gotta start young and teach that animals are not toys or a throwaway commodity, that when a dog gets old like Grandma and gets arthritis, it's not time to put them to sleep. That people need to love an animal until the end of its life. We're really trying," she said.

Stacey, a painter and geologist who used to work on rigs set against Colorado's majestic mountains, said that she recently received a call from her former employer to come back, but finds that she can't leave the shelter.

"I have to help these animals. It's hard, but I won't stop," she said. "As long as there's Clairol to cover up my grey hair, I'll be here."

***

"Kongs are the best things EVER!

Deuce is one of the lucky ones. The blue pit bull happily chewed his black Kong on the plush carpet at the Mobile home of April and Tony Durden, a young married couple and a Bama Bully Rescue foster family.

The two-year old dog was rescued from a Birmingham Shelter after scoring well on a temperament test. A sleek boy whose coloring would be referred to as "gunmetal gray" in the automotive world, Deuce's ears are mere nubs, a byproduct of a homemade crop job gone horribly wrong.

Extremely food motivated, Deuce temporarily controlled his manic juvenile energy to perform a trick.

April made Deuce stay for what must seem like forever to the canine. Deuce was almost trembling as she reminded him to slowly take back his Kong, which he did gently, as he did when he was rewarded with a treat.

"Deuce used to have resource aggression, but we're working it out," April said. "He'll be ready for a home soon. That's what we do at Bama. Prepare them for adoption, work out their issues in advance, so they're ready to be a part of their new family."

Finished, Deuce promptly ran up and down the hallway, a whirling dervish of wiggly pit bull excitement.

"Deuce should really be a service dog or a search and rescue dog," April noted. "He's just such a smart boy."

Tony and April had agreed to take Deuce in January after losing their beloved fawn colored pit bull named Roxy in December. Roxy is enshrined on a pillow on the overstuffed couch, her pink nose upturned, looking much like a solid caramel Loren and just as kissable.

"Roxy was my heart dog. I loved her more than anything," April said. "Even my mother, who didn't like pit bulls at first, came to love Roxy almost as much as I did."

April and I had met earlier that evening at Zoe's Kitchen, a fresh soup, salad, and generally healthy restaurant with an outdoor patio for Loren, who sat at my feet, tail wagging wildly as the band at the wine bar next store started playing. I smiled and pet the top of her head. My four-legged café society friend.

Loren soon attracted a teenage Zoe's employee, who rushed outside to greet her.

"Aaawww, you are so cute," the lanky blond girl said. "I just love you."

April observed her with an amused smile and a raised eyebrow.

"Do you know what kind of dog that is?" she asked sweetly.

"No, I can't tell," the girl answered, hugging Loren, who had jumped on her legs. "She's just sooo sweet."

"She's a pit bull," April said.

"Well, she's just great," the girl said, holding Loren's face between her hands and smooshing her wobbly cheeks. Loren rewarded her with several sloppy kisses on the nose.

Fishing out a card, April handed it to the girl. "Here. I'm with Bama Bully Rescue. Pit bulls need a lot of help in Mobile. You should talk to your parents, see if they'll let you foster one."

I grinned wryly. Rescuers.

The girl took the card. "I'll do that," she said, bounding back to the restaurant.

"Nice to meet you, April!"

April and Tony, both Alabama natives, are one of only two Bama Bully volunteer families in Mobile, so she was trying to increase local participation in their program. She also fielded calls from current pit bull owners who "needed" to give up their pet.

"So many people move without thinking of their dog. I can't imagine ever doing that," she said. "It's like, hey dumb ass, you didn't know you were moving? You couldn't have found a dog-friendly apartment?" A roll of the eyes.

I laughed and wasn't surprised later on to find out that tell-it-like-it-is April and I share the same birthday, though I originally pegged her for an Aries, a sign that is notoriously blunt.

April had long dark hair in braids that hung down her ample frame, almost to the middle of her back, and wore jean short overalls to ward off the heat. She could have still passed for a teenager, though she was in her mid-twenties.

April squinted in the sun, toying with the straw in her diet soda, and continued. "Tony and I can't have kids. I think God did that so I could serve the dogs. I can make a bigger difference in the world this way," she said softly. "It's fine with me. Dogs are the best. They don't tell me I'm fat. My nephew told me I was, but my dog never would."

***

The next day was devoted to playing tourist, so we drove through the ritzy part of Mobile, on Government Road, which was lined with mansions, huge brick estates with pillars and mammoth wrought iron fences like something out of a romance novel or *Gone with the Wind*.

Loren sat in the front seat and I grabbed her chin dramatically toward me. "With God as my witness, I will never go hungry again," I said and laughed at my incredible wit.

She looked at me, unimpressed, before returning to the scenery whizzing by outside her window. If Loren were my kid, I imagined she'd roll her eyes and say, "Whatever."

Intrigued by a cannon in the middle of an intersection, we stopped and went for a 15-minute walk at Memorial Park, which had a plaque dedicated to mothers of soldiers in the south. I took photos of Loren with the American flag waving proudly behind her, both beautiful sights.

I had scoped out dog friendly places online beforehand and was thrilled to find Café 615 on Dauphin Street, which is the main street in downtown, a charming mixture of history and commerce, lined with independent restaurants and shops. Rounding the corner, we came upon a well-shaded, beautiful brick patio with just one other party eating there.

We took the back corner so Loren would have some shade. Our waitress Kelly brought her a bowl of cool water and laughed when I ordered Loren a sliced, grilled chicken breast.

"Really?" she said, raising an eyebrow.

I nodded, looking down shyly. I realized this may have seemed frivolous to some.

"You're so funny," Kelly said. Turned out she was a dog lover and had many of her own, plus other critters such as lizards, cats, and guinea pigs her kids helped take care of. Kelly was looking for a home for the puppy she'd rescued a few months before, as she was moving in with a boyfriend who had two chocolate labs. She had advertised the puppy in her local paper, but hadn't had any hits yet.

"You're not going to turn her in to the shelter, are you?" I asked anxiously.

"Oh, no. I would never do that. That's why I took her in the first place," she replied. "If I can't find her a home, then I guess we'll just have a lot of dogs…a lot of dogs." Smile.

The cook came out and asked if Loren would be interested in some roasted potatoes they had left over. I

"Potatoes are not a part of my diet…"

thought she would, but the diva actually ate every bit of her chicken and left all the potatoes behind.

I, however, polished off my plate of an open-faced lump crab sandwich with creamy dill sauce and broiled Swiss cheese, plus a side salad of greens tossed with blueberries, roasted pumpkin seeds and gorgonzola in a light vinaigrette. It's seafood country here and I was taking full advantage. The salad was for health reasons.

Folk music played in the background. *I'll Have to Say I Love You* by Jim Croce, sappy tunes by John Denver, *The Boxer* by Simon and Garfunkel. Inexplicably, I started getting tears in my eyes. Then *Imagine* by John Lennon came on and I started crying at the table, which caught me totally off guard. I had been enjoying the perfect weather, Loren seemed content at my feet, the food was delicious. It was a window of grace, but it was mixed with sadness.

I tried to "imagine" a better world for the creatures I loved so dearly. I took action to make it a reality, yet sometimes, it was hard to visualize a time when the madness would stop. Right then, I imagined, there were millions of animals suffering and I felt a heavy weight on my heart to tell their story and do them justice. All this ran through my mind as I simultaneously enjoyed an exquisitely beautiful moment.

As The Verve song goes, "It's a bittersweet symphony, that's life..."

**

It struck me as we were driving back to our hotel and I saw a sign for Montgomery. We were in the deep South, the place I read about in social studies and history class as a kid, about Martin Luther King, about segregation, about police dogs and sit ins. This was the real deal. I let out a little gasp at the notion and found myself in gratitude for being able to take this trip.

For dinner, I consulted my handy *Roadfood* book and programmed Gidget for a popular BBQ joint just a few miles down the road. The parking lot was awash in delicious, tantalizing smoke. We pulled into a shady spot in the back and I went in to order. With a camera around my neck. Like a total geek tourist. The order placed, I started perusing all the reviews hanging on the walls when a man wearing sauce-stained scrubs poked his head out from the kitchen.

"Someone got a dog out there?"

Oh, God. "Yeah...what's wrong?"

He smiled. "Your dog's done up to jump out the window. She's setting off the alarm," he said. I started panicking about the exit and he directed me to the employee area. "You can come out this way."

I ran out to greet my nemesis, the diva, who was sitting upright in the driver's seat. I clicked off the alarm and sighed.

"It's great to travel with a dog and it's a pain to travel with a dog," I told the man. "You got dogs?"

"Yeah," he said. "Two pits."

I smiled.

"She a pit?" he asked me.

"Yeah. You want to meet her?" I asked.

"Yeah."

Loren jumped out and jumped all over him, but the man quickly asserted himself as alpha and Loren promptly straightened up from class clown to obedient student.

"She a red-nose?" he asked me.

"Not sure. More like a pink nose," I said. "Loren's from a shelter originally, but has been in rescue for the past few years. I imagine she's a mix. What about yours?"

"Mine are Boudreaux and Chinamen," he said proudly.

"Really?" I said, nodding. I had no idea what that meant. "That's cool."

He went back in to work and I sat in the parking lot with Loren, unwrapping the sandwich which, to my surprise, was served on thick, white bread rather than a bun. The smoky aroma permeated the incredibly soft meat, which was enhanced with a spicy, vinegar-based sauce. I gave Loren a few pieces without sauce, which she gently accepted. Still, she's no pig, like the Labs I've had over the years who were relentless once they smelled food. Loren waited patiently, never lowering herself to overtly beg.

Later on, I mentioned my new BBQ friend to a rescuer who specialized in pit bulls. She informed me that Boudreaux and Chinamen are lines of pit bulls descended from breeders in the south. Breeders that were known for fighting.

"That guy's dogs probably aren't pets," she said.

***

A huge thunderstorm ushered us out of Alabama and into Florida. This was a storm unlike anything I'd ever seen in California, a THX-Surround Sound, cracking, splotching, lightning-filled stunner that kept me in fear behind the wheel for two hours, going 35 to 40 MPH at some points on the highway, much of which was bridges built over dark, swirling water, just like Louisiana.

The sun started poking out around 45 miles from Panama City Beach. We pulled up to our campground in fine spirits. I had given myself a pep talk that I *could* indeed put up a tent and that we *were* going to enjoy roughing it.

The kind campground officers, Pam and Donna, assured me that St. Andrews State Recreation Area was a safe, fun park. This after Loren had jumped into Pam's cart and tried somewhat successfully to make out with her, which Pam was a good sport about.

"Are there alligators around here?" I asked.

They looked at each other, then at me. "Yeah," Pam said, polite enough not to add "duh, you're in Florida" to her response.

"Like, in the campground?" I continued.

"Well, they usually don't go into the campground, but they're sometimes on the outskirts. Just look out for them around bodies of water," Pam replied casually. She had her arm draped around Loren.

Umm, hello...usually?

I sucked it up, determined not to let this info freak me out. We hopped in the truck and went to space 32, which was conveniently located near the beach, with a beautiful view. Problem: no shade. *Except for a little patch in swampy grass near a body of water.* This simply wouldn't do for me or Loren. Both of us are fair and sunburn pretty easily, not to mention the possibility of being eaten alive by a huge reptile. Forget that night…what would we do for the 12 hours we were hit by direct sunlight the next day?

I went back to Donna and asked for a shady spot. Problem: campground was full. She suggested I go to Kmart and buy a tarp. I got in my truck, turned on the AC, fired up the laptop and frantically looked for hotels online instead, then decided to go for a drive to see them firsthand.

First, we stopped by the campground beach so Loren could see the water. I wasn't sure if she'd ever been to the beach before. That's when I saw the "no pets allowed" sign. Brilliant. In my infinite wisdom, I had picked an oceanfront town that doesn't let dogs on the beach.

"Great planning, Sathe," I said out loud. I looked around and since no one else was near the beach, took Loren out on the fine-grained white sand for a photo opp, the green-blue water providing a nice contrast behind her. Illegal, maybe, but we came all the way from California, ya know?

According to my web search, there were a lot of rooms available on the shorefront for $200 a night and up. Surprisingly, for the price, most of them looked abysmal, though they had merry seafaring names. We spent another hour and a half cruising for a bargain off from the beach. No such luck.

A more luxurious chain a mile and a half from the beach was available, so I plunked down twice as much as I wanted to spend. The room was plush, comfortable, and came with a big, wide desk for me to work on. As I updated the blog, the diva passed out on the comfortable, overstuffed couch.

I lied about Loren's breed when checking in, writing down boxer/pit bull mix. Why? I was afraid they wouldn't let us in a fancy place if I stated pit bull. I was kind of ashamed of myself, really. The next time, I vowed, I'd be 100 percent honest and proud to write pit bull, damn the consequences.

Frustrated, tired, and a little bummed that I was going over budget on this leg of the trip, I fed Loren, then took her for a walk, noticing a large, dark object off in the grass near the hotel. It was immobile and most likely a piece of wood rather than an alligator, but I stayed far from it and went toward the light in the parking lot.

Now it was time to feed me. I had spotted a little fresh fish market and restaurant up and across the street. Barnacle Bruce's. There was a lady sitting out front when we pulled up.

She was the manager and greeted us warmly, encouraging me to bring Loren on the patio. A lovely surprise awaited us. Around the corner from the modest storefront was a bit of peaceful paradise with a colorful garden, soothing water fountain, and a fresh floral scent in the air.

A woman and her daughter spotted Loren as they came out of the building next door.

"Is he mean?" the lady asked.

"No, she's really friendly. Come over and pet her," I said. Loren wagged her tail frantically against the post - thwack, thwack, thwack - in anticipation.

The mom and daughter bent down. Loren sniffed them both gently and bestowed a kiss on their noses. The little girl sat on a makeshift couch and Loren jumped into her lap as if she were a Yorkie rather than a 60-pound pit bull.

They were followed by a shirtless, tattooed surfer who came over to pet Loren. We chatted for a minute. He had returned to Florida from California, but left his heart near San Francisco. When I mentioned Loren was from California, he said, "Well, that just makes her even cooler."

"Who says I'm not a lap dog?"

I marveled at Loren's ability to make us friends. No one ever just came up to me and started talking. What a blessing she was. How impossibly lonely I'd be without her.

My order came up, a half pound of steamed Cajun shrimp, a half dozen oysters baked with butter, garlic and parmesan and a Greek house salad with pepperoncinis, olives, and tomatoes. The seafood was fresh, succulent, sweet and spicy, and I ripped the shells off the shrimp with primitive abandon, then licked my fingers clean. No one but Loren was watching.

Sherry, our waitress, had several rescue dogs of her own, and mentioned a sister who volunteered at the local Humane Society.

"You should have seen the dogs here after Katrina hit," she said, placing her hands on her chest. "It was heart wrenching."

"I bet," I replied, briefly imagining the catastrophe, then blocking it from my mind.

I expressed my desire for Loren to get adopted when we returned, that I didn't want her to go back to a kennel after experiencing having her own person for seven weeks, that I was worried I might be doing her more harm than good, leading her on in a sense.

"I will pray for that tonight," Sherry said.

"Thank you," I said, touched, and promptly screamed. A huge black bug of some sort had landed on my arm and almost gave me a coronary. Sherry and a gentleman eating at a table across the patio laughed.

"I hate bugs," I told them. "I hate alligators. I think I'm in the wrong place. Hey, are there alligators in that pond out there?"

Pause.

"I can't tell you no," Sherry said.

"OK, I'm not down with that," I said. "We have our problems in California, but alligators and massive insects are not part of them."

Despite the possibility of being bug/reptile food, we returned to Barnacle Bruce's for dinner the next night. The food was too good and the people were too kind. We made it out unscathed.

* * *

The air was thick in Florida. We got up and went for a walk at 7:30 a.m. and the humidity hit us like a steam room. Within 30 seconds, my hair started to curl.

After taking advantage of the free breakfast, one of the perks of a pricey hotel, I set up Loren for a flea bath appointment. She'd been scratching a lot; this was bug country, for all creatures apparently. Beforehand, I was determined for us to see the ocean, so we headed for the one dog-friendly beach I could find online, near the Dan Russell City Pier, set smack dab in the heart of Panama City Beach.

While finding a parking spot, my friend Liz in Pine Mountain Club called to say she had walked my dogs and that they were doing well. Having to parallel park, I asked Liz to hold and threw the phone in the back cab. It fell into Loren's water dish and died. A classic Sathe move.

Undeterred, we hit the beach. Loren was panting within five minutes, way more interested in the nasty kelp beds than the pristine blue-green water. She ran from the waves, as gentle as they were. Thankfully, the fine white sand wasn't hot or we wouldn't have made it five feet.

As we ambled up the shore, a young black Great Dane with floppy ears ran over to meet Loren. Unlike my civic-minded self, his owner didn't have the dog leashed. Though the dog seemed friendly enough, I panicked, yanking Loren away, hoping the Great Dane would get distracted. No such luck.

He made contact and I lamely pulled out my air horn, which I had brought with me from the mountains, where it was kept on hand as a bear deterrent. The horn gave a barely perceptible fizzing sound instead of a full barrel shrill, since I hadn't used it in months. The Great Dane's owner retrieved him before any altercation happened. She must have thought I was nuts, standing there in a panic, armed with a can of silence.

I felt bad for not giving Loren a chance to interact with the dog. She didn't seem aggressive, just startled. Perhaps I should have allowed her the choice of whether she wanted to meet a new dog and acted accordingly, instead of freaking out and setting her up for failure. I was far from a pack leader at times.

Loren was dropped off at the Barks and Bubbles salon, where she ran off with Matthew the groomer with nary a glance backward. Such a hussy.

I had three hours to myself. Too bad half of them were spent trying to track down a non-existent AT&T store (thanks, Gidget!) and getting my oil changed. The remainder was spent at Sharkey's, a tourist trap with mediocre food, but the most bitchen beach views ever. Like real estate, this restaurant was all about location, location, location. In the lobby, there was a "Lobster Zone" game, like the toy retrieval version found at restaurants everywhere, only the prizes here were live crustaceans ready to be cooked up. It was $2 a try. I passed.

In between reading "Me Talk Pretty One Day," I watched leathery brown people basking in the sunlight and ate my dry fish tacos. I had an epiphany. I, like Loren, am not a beach girl. I used to be a faithful sun worshipper, lavishing on the baby oil and sizzling for hours, but now I'd much rather be somewhere cool, like the mountains where I live. The heat is too much for me. I, too, am a delicate flower.

For that reason, I decided to reroute away from some of the beach campgrounds we had originally booked and head into the country. Also, no camping, unless we could upgrade to cabins. As much as I'd like to be a handy, rough-it kind of girl, I had to admit. it just wasn't my nature. I like having a roof over my head and preferably plaster, not nylon, which is vulnerable to, say, gators.

I'm not a wimp. I live in bear country and have been within 100 yards of a mountain lion, only to hike the same trail the next day. I just like my comforts. I'm getting older, I told myself, I deserve it and so does Loren. She'd spent enough time outside in her kennel.

***

Our initial foray into Savannah, Georgia was not auspicious. It was one of those days where little to nothing went right.

Endless driving. Motel room that smelled like cat pee. Motel clerks unwilling to help. Trying to find a recovery meeting on a highway with no address. Finding said meeting 20 minutes before it starts. Dashing into a Chinese food place for dinner beforehand, thinking that would be my quickest bet. Marveling that it took 15 minutes to make one order of Egg Foo Yung. Slopping said Egg Foo Yung down shirt and all over passenger seat in desperate attempt to finish in five minutes. Burning roof of mouth. Walking in late. Running out repeatedly when Loren set off the car alarm, no less than five times in 45 minutes, during an epic Southern rainstorm. Trying to sleep when the atmosphere was wet and heavy with humidity, despite the rumbling air conditioner.

Through it all, Loren was a trooper. She never complained. I would have complained if I'd been her. "This sucks. This room smells. I don't want Chinese food." Etc. That is why I took this trip with a dog. I knew there would be times that wouldn't be so joyous, times when things went wrong, when things would become downright irritating, which become exponentially worse with another frustrated human being by your side. Loren is almost unfailingly polite, except when she's tracking a new smell or sees a squirrel.

The next day was much better. We checked out of our hotel and found a cleaner one closer to the city. Top on our agenda was having lunch at Uncle Bubba's Oyster House (Bubba is Paula Deen's brother) with Mark and Julie Trexler, family friends that go back over 20 years. They are originally from the south, but lived in California for a few years. Mark, Julie, and their daughters, Ashley and Marianne, were a welcome part of many of my own family's vacations, camping trips, and barbecues throughout my teens and early twenties. It must've been over a decade since I'd seen them last.

They looked great, still youthful and happy, pulling up on their Harley Davidson, which has seen the Trexlers through 45 states. Mark is a high-level furniture manufacturing executive, which has afforded them a very nice life-style. They greeted Loren warmly, arranging for a table on the patio so she could join us.

It was perfect. We had a little private shaded area all to ourselves, over-looking the shallow tides. A guitarist played classic rock, serenading us with Jimmy Buffett and Van Morrison songs. The wait staff loved Loren, coming over to meet her and share their stories, from the waiter with the rescued black lab puppy to the waitress with a new bulldog "grandson."

Mark ordered us two dozen steamed oysters as a starter. They were fresh from Galveston, their rough shells the size of flattened tennis balls. Thankfully, Mark knew what he was doing, shucking them for both of us. Topped with lemon juice, hot sauce, and a little melted better, the oysters were divine; briny, succulent and very easy going down. They were a great counter-part to the complimentary, crumbly little cornbread cakes, which were so moist they didn't need any butter.

When it came around, I could barely tackle the huge bowl of shrimp and grits I ordered, an amazing dish: rich, creamy, studded with bits of smoky bacon, peppers, and onions, and overflowing with tender grilled shrimp. I sighed, looking at the task in front of me.

"I don't think I should've eaten so many oysters," I said. (Not to mention the cornbread.)

"Just eat the shrimp," Julie encouraged me. I did. Every single one. Gulf shrimp are light years ahead in taste from the farmed kind you might buy in grocery stores, which are usually imported from other countries. They're large, plump and juicy, bursting with fresh, sweet, salty goodness.

Between being treated to all that tasty food, about a gallon of Arnold Palmers, good conversation, and the relaxing vibe, I was feeling much better about life. So was Loren. She napped most of the time, stretching out on a shady part of the wooden deck.

"Dogs sleep about 20 hours a day," Mark noted.

So true. When I first started working from home, as a freelance publicist in 2007, I was shocked at how much my dogs slept. Loren was no exception. She napped whenever possible; in the car, at the hotel, under shady trees and bushes. When dogs are on, they're at 200 percent, so I presumed it must be exhausting.

Like when Loren spotted the tiny orange and grey Uncle Bubba's house cat. Suddenly, she was up on all fours, straining against her leash, wanting to, umm, introduce herself. Actually, she wanted the cat steamed with a side of melted butter. Thankfully, Loren was easily distracted, going over to Mark for attention and becoming fixated on something below our patio table before splaying out again.

After saying our goodbyes, Loren and I drove over the bridge to Fort Pulaski. Though I'm not a history buff, I couldn't help but be humbled by the thought of the men who died there in many a gruesome fashion, right on that soil. There was a huge brick fort, with cannons on the rooftop, and that famous Southern murky water filled the moat, where I imagined gators lurked beneath.

Loren and I sat under a tree for a few minutes, taking the scenery in. All that humidity produced some beautiful landscape. Grass as far as the eye can see, moss dripping from branches, swollen treetops swaying in the wind. Not too far from the fort was shoreline, where three men fished for their night's dinner under puffy white clouds and a cerulean blue sky.

Next, we took a brief jaunt to Tybee Island, a seaside town rife with tanned young bodies, families overloaded with beach gear, dune buggy and moped rentals, and lovely beach houses ranging from funky to palatial. I was so full, I managed to bypass a homemade ice cream shop, something that wouldn't usually be within my willpower.

We had one last stop to make before going back to our hotel. My car was making loud squealing noises, what I thought was my back brakes. When we pulled up to the auto repair shop, the mechanic took one listen and said, "That's your U joint."

That meant a $300 repair and three hours to fill the next day. Oh, well. We'd make the best of it. I was just glad the prognosis wasn't worse. My Toyota had more than 200,000 miles on it and had yet to have a major repair.

***

Loren and I were dropped off at River Street around 10:30 by a mechanic, who drove my truck back to the shop. We set off for the waterfront. The streets were rough, chunky old cobblestones with stone stairways so steep it took your breath away, literally and figuratively. Each road invariably led to architecture hundreds of years old and parks and memorials built at just about every corner.

We stopped to watch old-fashioned paddleboats meander along the river, tooting their horns. There were dozens of restaurants and gift shops that I wanted to explore, but really couldn't, as I wouldn't leave Loren tied up outside unattended. I didn't want her getting dog-napped. Strange logic, since they can't seem to give away pit bulls at shelters, but I wouldn't take any chances.

After walking a bit, we found The Dockside Restaurant toward the end of the riverfront. It not only had a shaded first-floor patio but misters to offset the heat. We made ourselves comfortable, me at the plastic table, Loren on the cool stone floor.

The crab chowder was pretty good, the overly sweet shrimp salad not so much. However, the homemade key lime pie was stellar; light, tart, creamy with a crumbly graham cracker crust. Very refreshing. Even better was the service. Our waitress, Melina, a young college-aged woman with long, curly reddish hair, sat with Loren twice while I went to the restroom. When I came back, Loren was being spoiled, her favorite activity.

"I have a red-nosed pit," Melina explained. "I bought her as a puppy from a breeder."

I raised my eyebrows, ready to launch into my standard lecture about adopting.

"I know," she held up a hand. "I was having second thoughts when I was there, but she was so sick and run down, I felt in my own weird way that I was rescuing her."

Loren the charmer had brought the hostess over a few times, too, who cooed at her. "I'm usually afraid of pit bulls, but this one's so sweet," I overheard her telling Melina.

The hostess also chastised people walking by with McDonalds cups. "Oh no, you did not come to Savannah, Georgia and have McDonalds for breakfast?" she said sweetly. Amen, sister. The thought alone was sacrilege to anyone who loves food.

There was a praline shop that caught my attention as we wandered back up the street, but when I heard some live music, it felt like a good time to take a break. The musician, a young, scruffy blonde man, was playing a banjo and harmonica simultaneously, singing songs from Sublime, Third Eye Blind, and to my surprise, Gloria Gaynor (*I Will Survive*). They all took on a Bob Dylan/*Deliverance* vibe which eventually grew monotonous, but for 15 minutes or so, I was utterly charmed and sang along, even getting teary-eyed at times. I was really getting sentimental in my old age.

The sun played on the water and I looked at my best friend at my feet, who panted happily as the river boats and crowds cruised by. I was stuffed full of tasty food and gratitude. Another moment of grace. I savored it.

A street artist named Levon came over to meet Loren and sell me a rose which he made from a native sugar palm leaf.

"What's your name?" he asked me after getting Loren's kissy-poo greeting.

"Michelle," I replied.

He smiled. He was missing four front teeth.

"Michelle! I've had experiences with Michelles. One that was great, one that was not so good," he said and looked me square in the eye. "You look like one of the good ones. I can tell."

I smiled. Levon, I'm sure, was a junkie. His eyes were glazed and yellow. His clothes and shoes were dirty, his black skin deeply leathered. Levon spoke in a shuffling cadence that I could barely understand as he quickly fashioned my rose with his rough hands, explaining each step. It was beautiful, intricately wound and finished with a wispy fluorish. The cost was $5.

"A special deal for you," Levon assured me.

Sure. I gave him $1 tip. We all have to make a living.

Loren and I made our way to a park. I laid down the hoodie I had tied around my waist as a blanket. At 1:30 p.m. I called the shop. The repairs would be another hour. We lounged and Loren made some new friends with the young children playing with their parents on the swings or slides nearby.

At 2:30 p.m. I called again. It would still be another half hour. I asked to be picked up and was told a mechanic would come get me. I pulled out a book and tried to get comfortable, but my butt hurt and my attitude was heading south from the heat and anxiety. Loren, however, looked on the whole episode as a prime opportunity to nap. Humans could learn a lot from dogs.

At 3 p.m., no mechanic and no contact. I rang the shop. The driver would be asked to call me back. At 3:15 p.m. I called again. The driver "had gotten into an accident." Was he freaking kidding me? Was this some weird form of Southern torture? You don't leave a California girl in a strange town without her car - that's like taking Linus' security blanket away. I was losing my patience.

"We can send a cab for you," I was told.

"I don't care who you send for me, just tell me who it is and when they're going to be here," I said.

"I'll call you back," the cashier said.

Surprise, just a few minutes later, my car was done and the mechanic who dropped us off picked us up. By this time, I was pretty wiped out and we had a two hour drive to Dublin, where Mark and Julie lived. I was so tired, I periodically slapped myself to stay awake until I found a station playing really bad 80s music, which kept me enthralled wondering how the hell these songs could have ever been hits. (There's a reason Taco's *Putting on the Ritz* is not in heavy rotation. My pick for worst 80s song, however, is *Safety Dance* by Wang Chung. Worst video, too.)

It was 7 p.m. when we pulled up to Mark and Julie's large, lovely two-story brick estate, set on seven acres of rolling green lawn, with a lake in the backyard. Loren ran right up to the front door as if to the manor born. Inside, she sniffed around incessantly, intensely preoccupied with some of the stuffed animals Mark had killed while hunting. Loren was especially interested in the massive wolf.

"If that wolf was alive, you wouldn't be so curious," Julie told her.

I don't like hunting, at least if you're not going to eat the meat. I'm pretty much a total lefty liberal, while Mark and Julie are conservatives, but we got along fine, even when conversation headed toward dangerous political territory. We just agreed to disagree and moved on.

After a delicious dinner of grilled chicken with a vinegar-based barbecue sauce, mozzarella, tomato, and avocado salad, grilled corn and roasted Vidalia onions (a special sweet variety native to Georgia), we went beyond their gorgeous property for a peek at their neighbor's homes.

Mark stopped at a fence and called to some horses in a yard. They came trotting over and I looked at Loren, wondering if she would try to attack them. She stood up on the fence with Mark, watching intently. It was quite a scene, with the sun setting in a pink and red blaze behind them. I could almost see the wheels turning in Loren's head as she stuck her blocky head through the posts to get a better look.

"These creatures are a lot bigger than me," she seemed to be thinking. "I better just let them be."

So she did, taking her head out of the posts and leaning it against Mark's hip for reassurance, still perched on her back legs, tail lightly waving back and forth.

"Wow, Winston would always bark at the horses," Julie said.

Winston was the Trexler's lab who died that March at the age of 13. I could tell Mark and Julie missed him, as well as Hewey, their female mutt, who had passed away just a few months before Winston. They treated Loren as if she were their own, constantly petting her and letting her kiss them.

"She's such a sweetie," they both said repeatedly.

We had a great night's sleep in the guest room, with some of the most divine pillows on earth, not getting up until 8 a.m. Julie and I had some cereal and a pleasant chat before I took a shower. Before I got in, I noticed Julie laying on the ground with Loren, stroking and talking to her. They were in the same position when I got out 20 minutes later.

"You could adopt Loren," I said hopefully, tentatively. "I'd be happy to deliver her to you after the trip."

"I wish we could," Julie sighed. "But we travel too much. It's not the right time."

***

We had 320 miles to Asheville, North Carolina from Dublin. The drive was gorgeous; Georgia's got grass for days and lush farmland for weeks. We stopped for peaches on Highway 441, at the only fruit stand that would sell me half a basket, and picked up some candied pecans and BBQ sauce, too. The peach was so juicy, its sweet nectar squirted all over my clothes and ran down my hand. I needed a bib. It was glorious.

When the mountains of Asheville came into view, with trees so dense they looked like a bunch of broccoli crowns in the distance, my heart skipped. It felt like home. Our hotel was tucked away in the woods, about a mile from the Blue Ridge Parkway entrance. It was a flat, sprawling, two-story circa the 1950s, but clean. The air was fresh and there were plenty of grassy areas for Loren to take potty breaks.

On a tip from my *USA* guidebook, we went to look for Early Girl Eatery in the downtown area. It was closed, but there was a patio at Market Place Restaurant right down the brick-lined street, set amongst dozens of boutiques and businesses. What a serendipitous find. A $29, three-course prix fixe menu that rocked my world.

First, a potato leek soup, light and springy with a drizzle of piquant pepper sauce, which when swirled into the soup, added a welcome bit of spice. The main course, a strip steak with blue cheese butter, came sliced and artfully arranged. It was even better than it looked, the meat expertly grilled medium rare and finished with a bit of sea salt, the savory butter melding into the meat, which swam in a sea of creamy cauliflower puree. I sighed with pleasure.

Loren, who was lounging on the brick floor, looked at me sweetly and I couldn't help myself; I sucked off the sauce and gave five little pieces to her.

Dinner was finished with a molten chocolate lava cake with ice cream, which of course, I did not share (chocolate can be fatal to dogs). I had to restrain myself not to lick the plate.

The chef, named Michelle, came out to greet us and I praised her effusively. It was so nice to see food this thoughtfully composed - especially from someone so young. Chef Michelle smiled shyly, graciously accepting my feedback. She squatted down to pet Loren and told me about her own dog, a young Australian shepherd.

"Someone dumped a box of 10 puppies on the road, where they weren't found for over a week," she said. "They were in pretty bad shape. I rescued one of them."

An awesome chef and a dog person. If I ever moved to Asheville, I vowed to make Michelle my friend.

***

I have a theory about vacations. The first third goes by in slow motion, the second third in real time, and the last third in fast forward. We were about one-third in and it seemed things were moving along at a much quicker pace.

We woke up at 9 a.m., way late for this early bird, but I had been up until 11:30 working on the blog the night before, so I was beat. We didn't leave for Blue Ridge Parkway until 11 a.m., after picking up a slice of vegetarian quiche, a double chocolate cookie, and some chai iced tea at Filo, an upscale bakery just a few blocks from our hotel.

It took about five miles for the scenery to get interesting, though a guy

"This is pretty and all, but the truck beckons…"

riding down the mountainside on a unicycle provided comic relief. Our first stop was at Bad Fork Valley, which had a 3,350 elevation and a panoramic view of the dense foliage. Loren became rooted to a cluster of succulent plants, sniffing away. Until the bees came in. Once she heard the buzz, Loren's ears went right up, her eyebrows furrowed and she ran, not walked, back to the security of the truck.

The truck chugged its way uphill. It was a Tuesday afternoon and I was seeing the Blue Ridge Mountains, one of the most magnificent sights in the whole country. I felt so peaceful and lucky. Loren snoozed in the back, as usual, missing the beauty but enjoying it all in her own way. Like a dork, I honked through every tunnel and there were a lot of them.

I was in awe over the work it must have taken to make this highway a reality, of the whole U.S. highway system and the many conveniences it provides for travelers. Having lived in Shanghai for 15 months in 1999 and part of 2000, where there were no bathrooms or gas stations outside any major city (and those in the city were often dirty troughs), I know how lucky we are in America.

I admired the many bicyclists on the road, pedaling with purpose up the hill and through the tunnels, outfitted with helmets and luminescent safety strips. Brave, hardy souls. I bet they didn't plan their vacations around food.

Cursed with the tiny Sathe bladder, within a half hour I was looking for a restroom. This trait generally annoys the hell out of human travel companions; I'm worse than a little kid. I saw the universal bathroom symbol and pulled over to the Mt. Pisgah pass. We had to hike a bit to get there, but thankfully the trail was shaded and cool, so Miss Thang made it with no problems.

Until we got to the restroom. Since other people were in the area and I refused to leave Loren alone, I dragged her in with me. And I mean drag.

"Come on, diva," I said. "I really have to go."

Loren shot me a look of annoyance and acquiesced, allowing me to lead her into the clean restroom. We went into the handicapped stall, which was spacious enough for both of us.

"Sorry, Loren. This is how humans do it. We can't just pee in the grass," I told her. "I wish we could."

She just looked at me for a second with big eyes and tried to crawl under the stall, far away from her crazy auntie.

At the 4,000 foot elevation range, the scenery shifted a bit, the broccoli crown clusters sprouting skinny pine trees that looked like asparagus stalks. Shades of pink and white imbued the flowers that grew at each stop. We stopped at Funnel Top, where I glimpsed the valley of trees below, and tried to get Loren to take a potty break or photo opp, but she wasn't having it. The clouds had opened up with a wallop and started raining.

"Are you crazy? It's wet out there," Loren seemed to say as I tried to coax her out of the truck. She stayed put. We went as far as the view sight for Cold Mountain (one of my favorite movies) before heading for city life again.

Gidget led us to the 151 on our way back, a tight, winding road with a canopy of trees that grew horizontally, as if to greet visitors. A smell of citrus permeated the air. Six miles from Asheville, neighborhoods started springing up, from tiny trailers to big, beautiful wood homes, some with horses grazing on their vast lawns. I watched an ancient Australian Shepherd amble across its spacious property and smiled.

I programmed Gidget to head to a bookstore, but was diverted by a Farmer's Market sign and ditched the plan. This wasn't your typical table and tent affair. Asheville's Farmer's Market is open daily, two massive metal buildings overflowing with vendors selling nuts, meats, cheeses, produce, honey, ice cream, fudge, and just about anything else you can imagine. There was even a drive-thru section with more produce and purveyors of plants under an industrial-sized carport.

I managed to escape that foodie paradise with a small purchase - a quart of strawberries, to be enjoyed for dessert that night and breakfast the next day, and $3 of cured meat similar to bacon that doesn't have to be refrigerated, according to Kevin, a vendor. I would bring it home to make authentic collard greens.

After chit chatting about where I was from and telling Kevin about our mission, he mentioned his sister had recently adopted a pit bull.

"She loves that dog. It's changed her life," he said.

I knew the feeling. Besides the love I had for my own pit mixes at home, I was becoming more enamored with Loren each day. I wondered if I were doing her more harm than good with this trip, perhaps making her believe she was my dog, only to take her back to The Brittany Foundation kennels.

I prayed that someone, maybe someone reading about our adventures online or in *The Signal*, would step up and give Loren the home she deserved, that we could choose from four or five quality people waiting to adopt her when we returned to California on July 4th.

Until then, I vowed to take it one day at a time and enjoy the incredible opportunity to see the country with such a fantastic friend by my side. One never knew what tomorrow might bring.

The next morning, during our last walk in the Asheville motel parking lot, I noticed a maid looking at Loren with a smile on her face.

"Want to meet her?" I asked.

Not that she had much choice. Loren was already on her way for an introduction, pulling me along for the ride.

"You've got a pretty dog," the maid said, leaning down and letting Loren kiss her.

"She's not my dog," I replied. "Her name's Loren and she lives at a no-kill rescue in California. We're just traveling across country together to promote animal adoption and pit bull awareness."

The maid's name was Amy and she was interested in adopting Loren. When she asked how much the fee was, I said $150 and she said that was a lot.

"There are plenty of dogs like Loren at local shelters looking for a family," I said. "They usually only charge $30 to $50 and they're fixed and everything."

Amy shook her head. "That's true," she said. "This one just seems like a real sweetheart."

She had OZZY tattooed on her left hand and more tattoos up her forearm and on her neck. My inner hesher grinned in recognition. Back in the day, I admired that look, I just never had the balls to get inked.

As we walked away, Amy called after us.

"That's a real awesome thing you're doing," she said.

I got tears in my eyes. "Well, she's an awesome dog," I stammered.

Michael Vick, Crab Cakes & Cheese Steaks

The majestic mountains of Asheville gave way to the pastoral rolling hills of Virginia, where the lush, grassy countryside was dotted with farmhouses, and church steeples were the only architecture interrupting the skyline. We were going to Wytheville, a one-night stop on the way to Baltimore.

It was beautiful, but as Wayde said to me the other night, "There's a price to pay for all that green." The price is lots of rain, kind of odd for June, at least where I'm from. A typical Southern California girl, I just assumed every day on this trip would be sunny, but brought along a few hoodies just in case.

We arrived in the early evening. Hungry, we cruised Wytheville's Main Street, where there were many red-brick and white-roofed churches but just a few restaurants, mostly closed. Wait…what was that in the distance? Dukes BBQ - "Best BBQ in Wytheville." Hmm.

It was pretty darn good…and cheap, only $3.99 for a pulled pork sandwich. The meat had a tender, melt-in-your-mouth texture and was smothered in a tangy sauce atop a soft egg bun. I pulled out my camera to take a photo of the sandwich for the blog before I demolished it. As I did so, I noticed I'd attracted a weird reaction from the two couples eating across from me.

"You wanna take our picture?" one of the women asked me sarcastically, followed by a high-pitched cackle. She had a really bad perm and sharp, pinched features, one of those girls who probably wasn't very popular in high school and made everyone pay for it the rest of her days.

"Um, no…I just like taking food pictures," I responded calmly, proud of myself for not adding "It's none of your f'ing business."

They all stared at me as if I were an alien life form and I continued snapping as they laughed. Whatever. A few minutes later, a pastor came to join them for dinner and once again I was struck by the hypocrisy of churchgoers who don't exactly practice what they preach.

I should sic Loren on them, I thought, and looked out to see her faithfully waiting for me in the truck, sitting in the passenger seat, her little red and white head staring intently into the window. As if she would do anything other than lick the idiots.

***

The diva wanted to sleep in, so we left for Baltimore at 10:15, an hour later than I'd intended, passing signs for dog race tracks. Those poor greyhounds, handled like livestock for most of their lives and dumped in shelters or killed en masse when they were no longer of service. They were probably right behind pit bulls in terms of mistreatment. Sigh. So many injustices in this world.

Stopping in Harrisburg to get gas, I let Loren out for a break. On our way to the grassy area, a woman with bleached blonde hair spotted Loren and made a scared noise, followed by an "Ooh…" which sounded more like boo, before she practically ran from us.

"She's friendly," I said.

She kept sprinting and made another "ooh…" this time with a disgusted look, which really pissed me off.

"God, she's just a dog!" I said and hurried along, as mad as a mother bear protecting her cub. It incensed me that people think they know Loren with one look. It's so ignorant. Especially since her demeanor is so gentle.

Once we were back in the truck, rolling along the highway, my blood pressure receded amongst the tranquil beauty. It shocked me to think this bucolic setting was also the backdrop for a notoriously violent crime scene, the Michael Vick dog fighting ring.

Grim, grainy images of pit bulls locked in mortal combat, bloodied and scarred, popped into my mind and made me shudder. The footage had been splashed for months across major news channels as the Vick case made national headlines. Ironically, as we drove along Virginia's highways, news radio buzzed with the latest on Vick, who was on the verge of release from jail and the possibility of being recruited back onto the football field.

***

Dog fighting traces back to 1835, when bull baiting was banned in England. Bulldog owners, who had previously used their dogs to bait bulls, bears, and other animals, turned to staging dog fights instead. Large, heavy bull dogs were bred with smaller, faster terriers to produce bull terriers. Staffordshire Bull Terriers, American Staffordshire Terriers, and American Pit Bull Terriers hail from this lineage. The Humane Society estimates that there are 30,000 to 40,000 active dog fighters in America today, despite its illegal status in all 50 states, many of which consider it a felony.

On December 10, 2007, Vick, the hotshot quarterback for the Atlanta Falcons, was convicted for participating in a dog fighting conspiracy that involved gambling and the killing of pit bulls, and was sentenced to 23 months in prison. He had turned himself in to authorities on November 19, 2007, following a guilty plea to a federal dog fighting charge on August 27.

It was a change of heart for the football star, who had originally denied all involvement with dog fighting. The charges came when authorities, tipped off by a relative of Vick's friend, searched his Surry County property for drugs on April 26. Instead, they found 66 dogs, 55 of those pit bulls, and dog fighting paraphernalia that included a rape stand (for breeding unwilling females), pry bar, treadmill and a bloodied piece of carpet. Typical of dog fighters, Vick kept half the dogs tethered to car axles with heavy chains, which allowed the dogs to get close to each other, but not to have contact, a very effective recipe for aggression.

On April 27, Vick released a statement saying he was never at the house and blamed family members for taking advantage of his generosity. The following day, he met with NFL commissioner Roger Goodell to discuss the investigation. According to reports, Vick continued to plead his innocence. In May, however, an informant told ESPN that Vick was a dog fighting "heavyweight" back in his college days, when he used to bet large sums on the matches. In June, officials obtained another search warrant for Vick's property, where they found the remains of seven dogs.

The unsettling news began a series of corporate and public relations repercussions against Vick, including the loss of his AirTran Airways endorsement and the cancellation of an appearance at a William & Mary football camp. Nike, however, announced it had no plans to drop its sponsorship of the NFL star.

An 18-page indictment by a federal grand jury on July 17 introduced a rough timeline of how dogs were electrocuted, drowned, shot or hanged at Bad Newz Kennels on the Surry County property, which it stated was founded in 2002 by Vick and three co-defendants Tony Taylor, Purnell A. Peace, and Quanis L. Phillips. With purses allegedly as high as $26,000, Bad News Kennels regularly attracted competitors from seven surrounding states.

Harrowing information on the operation emerged, such as the scratch marks on the inside of the property's pool, where dogs frantically tried to escape from drowning. Another account stated that after being consulted, Vick ordered Peace to kill a female pit bull after losing a fight. "She's got to go," Vick was reported to have said. Further reports indicated that Vick would sometimes throw dogs that were family pets into the ring, where they would often die.

July continued to be a bad month for Vick, who was ordered to stay away from the Falcons training camp and was under consideration for suspension while the NFL conducted their own investigation. Despite his not guilty pleas on July 26, Nike suspended its contract with Vick and pulled goods bearing his name off their Nike store shelves. At court appearances, the football star was roundly booed by animal rights protestors and dog lovers, many with signs that bore disturbing photos of four-legged dog-fighting victims.

On July 30, Taylor entered a guilty plea, followed by Peace and Phillips in mid-August. On August 23, Vick formally entered a plea agreement, where he admitted to conspiracy in the dog fighting ring and helping to kill pit bulls. Later that day, the NFL announced it had suspended Vick indefinitely.

Animal welfare groups differed on what to do with the former Vick dogs, who were being kenneled at a Virginia shelter. The Humane Society of the United States and PETA wanted them killed, which up to that point was routine practice for fighting dogs. Pit bull advocacy groups such as San Francisco's Bad Rap wanted them rescued and rehabilitated by qualified organizations.

Setting a stunning precedent, U.S. District Judge Henry E. Hudson ordered that the dogs not be judged by their breed stereotype and instead be evaluated individually. He also ordered Vick to pay almost $1 million for the lifelong care of the dogs that could be saved. Evaluated by animal behavior experts in the fall of 2007, only one of the 49 Vick pit bulls was deemed too vicious to warrant saving and was killed; another was euthanized due to illness.

Twenty-four of the 47 surviving dogs were placed directly in foster homes through Bad Rap and an undisclosed East Coast rescue group. Many went on to live with other dogs, some even with cats. Jonny Justice, a spunky black and white male and Bad Rap alumni, is a Canine Good Citizen and helps young children learn how to read. Leo, a tan muscular male, was taken in by Our Pack in Sacramento and serves as a therapy dog to comfort hospitalized cancer patients.

**

Georgia rolled around on her back in the brick-red dirt of Kanab, Utah. There was a wide toothless grin on her scarred face as she wiggled with her stomach exposed, awaiting the inevitable rubs from John Garcia, co-manager of Dog Town at Best Friends Animal Sanctuary and star of the TV show of the same name (which aired on the National Geographic channel from 2007 - 2010).

Garcia watched the dog's antics with a wide grin. "When she first came here, Georgia didn't like people. You couldn't touch certain parts of her body," Garcia said. "Now it's just belly rubs and kisses."

The pit bull was one of the 22 Vick dogs brought back to Best Friends in December, 2007, for rehabilitation. These were mainly the older dogs or harder-luck cases deemed the most difficult to turn around.

When Garcia met Georgia during the assessment phase in Virginia, a kennel worker told him that Georgia didn't care about humans and would never become rehabilitated. Initially Georgia wouldn't make eye contact with Garcia and even growled at him, but Garcia kept moving forward. About halfway through the assessment, the pair made eye contact and Georgia's aggression melted away.

"I was surprised that the judge ruled in the dogs' favor. I'm not aware of dog fighting bust dogs that had ever been allowed into rescue before," Garcia said. "Obviously, we wanted to save their lives, but we also knew it was an opportunity to educate the public and show people they could be rehabilitated."

Known formerly as Jane, Georgia was one of Vick's prize fighters and breeders, a sad history that's readily apparent from the deep, dark grooves and scratches slashed indiscriminately across her rust-colored face and body, which also bears large, black nipples from her distended stomach.

Despite her less-than-perfect appearance, Georgia has blossomed into a canine celebrity, with many media appearances under her belt; she and Garcia have been featured on *Larry King Live*, *Ellen* and too many print publications to mention. She is particularly famous for bestowing her trademark kisses on unsuspecting crew members and reporters; a video of her attempting to make out with ESPN reporter Tom Forrey is a hit on You Tube.

"She gives very unique kisses, since she has no teeth and her tongue hangs out on the side of her mouth," Garcia said with affection.

According to Garcia, the Vicktory dogs, as they had been dubbed by Best Friends, began to make the transformation from victims to victorious after about a month at the sanctuary, though they showed signs of improvement right away.

Meeting Georgia and John Garcia at Best Friends

Upon arriving in Southern Utah after their long journey from Virginia, each dog was released into a pen in Dogtown. Toys began flying in the air, water buckets were knocked over, and a rash of zoomies, or running around in tight, fast circles that Garcia noted "pits do the best," broke out.

"They had been products of a stressful environment before, so now they were just doing what came naturally," Garcia said. "I think they knew we were here to help."

Staffed with five full-time trainers, kennel management, and countless volunteers, Dogtown is a series of 37 octagon-shaped buildings set on vast acreage at the sanctuary. Each individual run has a weatherproof enclosure with a doggy door that leads to a large, fenced outdoor area. Also at Dogtown is the Best Friends veterinary clinic, where the sanctuary's approximately 2,000 animals (horses, pigs, birds, cats, dogs, and some wildlife) are treated and the public is offered low-cost spaying and neutering.

Several of the Vicktory dogs suffered from medical ailments, usually a result of bad breeding or neglect, that Garcia felt contributed to their temperament issues. Denzel, a handsome black male with white swirls on his chest, almost died during a tooth extraction when he wouldn't stop bleeding from a disorder that thinned his blood. Others had to have knee replacements due to dysplasia.

"You know how when humans don't feel well, they're snappy? It's the same thing with dogs," Garcia said.

The Vicktory dogs were also DNA tested to determine their lineage. To Garcia's surprise, most of the dogs were found to be mixes, showing secondary or just trace amounts of American Pit Bull Terrier; only Layla, Georgia, and Ray Ray were primarily purebred pit bulls.

While many of Dogtown's residents are paired with other dogs, the Vicktory dogs were initially kept separated due to their history. Daily reports began on the dogs activities and behaviors, which included learning how to walk on a leash, going for car rides into town, and socializing with humans, often through overnight stays with staff.

Slowly, they also became socialized with other dogs through gradual introductions. Today, many live in pairs, though some, like Georgia, still prefer their space. The staff has worked with Georgia so that she can now tolerate other dogs within leash distance, rather than wanting to attack from a hundred yards away, as was her nature when she arrived at Best Friends.

To be considered for adoption, per court order, the Vicktory dogs have to be in foster care with the potential adopter for six months and acquire their Canine Good Citizen certification during that time. Extensive background checks are also required on the adopters.

Halle, a pert, pouty black female, was the first Vicktory dog to find her forever home. She now shares couch time with Tacoma, another Best Friends bully rescue, and their human mom Traci (last names and locations of Vicktory dog adopters are held in confidence). Photos show Tacoma with his arm protectively curled around Halle, who snuggles deep into his barrel chest.

Traci educates her community about pit bulls by taking the pair out and setting up a small sitting area with signs that read, "Would you like to pet me and learn more about me? Please just ask."

To get ready for his family, Handsome Dan, a buff tan male, was first taken for a series of overnight stays where he could become acclimated to the many sights and sounds found in a home.

"We introduced him to hardwood floors, mirrors and anything else that he might find traumatic. It doesn't matter what breed a dog is if they are under socialized," Garcia said. "When Handsome Dan went into his new home, he walked in as if he owned the place."

The Vicktory dogs' successes continued to unfold on "Dogtown," and Garcia credited the show with an increase in volunteerism at Dogtown, as well as an increased acceptance of the pit bull breed.

"Our fan mail has been amazing. Most people don't automatically believe pit bull equals vicious dog anymore," he said. "Any positive media has been a bonus for these dogs."

Ironically, it all stemmed from an incredibly negative beginning, which Vick has diligently tried to turn around as the new Humane Society spokesman against dog fighting, a move that some animal welfare activists dismissed as a public relations campaign to get him back in the NFL. (Vick was signed to a two-year contract by the Philadelphia Eagles in August 2009.)

Garcia remained neutral on the topic, but gave Vick credit for inadvertently helping the breed he once sought solely to destroy.

"I definitely think Michael Vick has brought awareness. People know now dog fighting is illegal, instead of merely looked down upon," Garcia said. "Honestly, I can't speak to whether Vick's sincere or not, but I hope he sticks to the track he says he's on. He's part of the culture of the inner city. He could be very helpful."

***

Say the name Michael Vick to kids in South Central Los Angeles, one of the areas served by the non-profit Downtown Dog Rescue, and the response is swift and vociferous.

"The kids, and by that I mean young men from 13 to their early 20s, love him," said Downtown Dog Rescue founder Lori Weise. "I hear them say, 'Michael Vick says don't fight dogs, I won't fight dogs.' When I told them I was working with the Humane Society to bring him to our class, you would have thought Obama was coming."

The majority of them, according to Weise, feel Vick was framed, a victim himself of an unscrupulous entourage that didn't have his back and a society eager to persecute a successful young black man.

"I remain neutral and listen to the debates, which are so well argued that if I were from another country and had never heard of Michael Vick, I would understand their point of view," Weise said.

Originally founded in 1996 to help dogs owned by the homeless population of Skid Row, Downtown Dog Rescue began to change its focus upon the gentrification of the area. Now they serve South Central, Watts, and Compton, low-income, high-minority communities where pit bulls are prevalent and dog fighting is an everyday occurrence.

Weise has been witness to spontaneous bouts on street corners, alerted first by the horrifying sounds of strong beasts locked in mortal combat - growling, crying, whining, teeth ripping flesh-followed by the cheers of 20-30 residents watching it all go down. It's disturbing, but a far cry from the highly-structured, big-money fights like those of Bad Newz Kennels.

"That kind of dog fighting is really an organized crime, it doesn't go on here very often. If it does, it's so secretive that none of my guys are hooked into it or if they were, they would never let me know until way after the fact," Weise said.

Her "guys" are gangbangers and street thugs, the kind of young men reported about nightly on the 11 o'clock news, as well as those simply caught in the crossfire of a poverty-stricken life that offers few options out of the neighborhoods. They are mostly black and Latino, both cultures that have embraced dog fighting over the generations, as Weise illustrated.

"It's something you grow up with. If your dad and uncle went to dog fights, you're probably going to do it, too," Weise said. "It makes them feel powerful. It's an adrenaline rush."

Pit bulls are the dog of choice on these streets, whether it's for fighting, breeding, or keeping in the backyard or on a chain for protection. They are overflowing the city and county shelters, followed closely by Chihuahuas, according to Weise. "Usually, the pit bull is the yard dog and the Chihuahua is the house pet," she said.

Weise does her best to rescue and rehabilitate pit bulls from the system or from Downtown Dog Rescue clients that can no longer keep their pets. Currently, Weise has 21 dogs, primarily bully breeds, living at the rescue's kennels located behind her downtown L.A. furniture factory. The business had brought her to the area. A pit bull named Iron Head and his owner Benny started her on the rescue path.

The duo shared a cardboard box in an alley, outfitted with makeshift bunk beds (Benny slept on top) and a small book case. Over time, Weise noticed the connection between Benny and Iron Head, a gentle, massive dog who would happily amble off-leash by his owner's side.

"Benny would talk to Iron Head like he was his son," Weise said. "I began talking to Benny about the dog. I never had an experience talking to a homeless person before, except when they asked for money."

When Iron Head had puppies with a female stray, Weise took action, first finding homes for the litter, then getting Iron Head neutered. Since Benny was reluctant to do the surgery, Weise snuck the dog into a veterinarian while his owner was on an errand, leaving behind a note that Iron Head would be back in a few days.

Benny began to appreciate what he called "Miss Lori's thing," and started working with Weise to get other homeless-owned dogs fixed, giving her street credibility in the process. "They would be nervous, wondering if they could trust me to bring their dog back. All I had to say was I was a friend of Benny's and they would be in," Weise said.

Weise applied for non-profit status and began receiving funds through private donations and government grants, which allowed her to create spay/neuter programs and provide veterinary care and dog food to those in need in order to prevent owner surrenders.

"Once they go to a shelter, it's all downhill," Weise said. "Close to 90 percent of pit bulls in Los Angeles shelters are euthanized."

Downtown Dog Rescue networks available dogs on their website and through outreach to other rescues, resulting in the adoption of 150 to 250 dogs annually. The organization partnered with The Amanda Foundation for a free mobile spay/neuter clinic that has fixed thousands of dogs in areas usually ignored by animal control, despite Los Angeles' mandatory spay/neuter ordinance.

"There's certain areas that I honestly think animal control officers, if they spoke candidly and off the record, would tell you that they're scared to go into. When I go in, I'm not causing any problems or fining anyone, we're offering free stuff. We're the good guy," Weise said. "We'd see less abuse if we'd ask how we could help the community and bring resources to them, instead of calling them the problem."

DDR's Safety Net was launched in December 2008 with help from the City and County of Los Angeles. The program offers resources to owners for keeping their dogs in the home, including a hotline which logged 22 calls in one week, ranging from an owner that needed help for her dog with mange to another owner who just wanted to talk to someone about her leash-aggressive dog, which friends and neighbors had encouraged her to get rid of.

Weise got some medication for the former and listened to the latter, then offered some training tips. Each owner left happily from the exchange and two more dogs were saved from the system.

"We do what works for this demographic. These are people that don't have Twitter or Facebook. We do it the old-fashioned way, distributing flyers and placing a listing in throwaway newspapers like the *Pennysaver*. Most of our clients come from word of mouth like 'My cousin used your service and he was happy,'" Weise said.

On Sundays, Downtown Dog Rescue offers free training classes for dog owners at the Los Angeles Coliseum. Attracting 20 to 50 attendees, the class runs through basic skills such as sit, stay, come, and walking on a leash properly, as well as promoting socialization between the dogs. Owners with aggressive methods are called out by trainers, who invite them for further training at Private 101 classes. For fun, the group practices agility at the facility's many tables and benches. The four-legged students are primarily pit bulls.

Through her many different efforts, Weise has created an underground network of street volunteers who bring a unique set of skills to the table. One man, a former pit bull breeder, combs the streets with Weise to convince others to stop the practice and have their animals fixed at mobile spay/neuter clinics.

"He'll act as kind of a bodyguard when I go to look at a situation. If we cruise by and check out a house and he says, 'Nah ah, we're not stopping here,' I'll let it go," Weise said.

Weise cultivated his trust over the years by providing access to underground veterinary services for what she suspected were fighting dogs, never asking any questions, giving the man food for neighborhood dogs in need and whatever else she could do. Finally, after years of this and of seeing more and more aggressive dogs being bred together to create what she termed "the ultimate fighting machines," Weise said she had enough and told the man she needed him on her team, that she just couldn't do it alone anymore.

"He could see, I am serious about this, that I'm not leaving, that I'm embedded in community," Weise said. "We were both sick of the shit going on, sick of seeing the dogs coming to our class torn up, one hit so hard in the head that the eye had detached from his retina."

With a 50 percent and climbing high school drop-out rate in Los Angeles, racial profiling, often tragic home lives, and a blatant lack of educational or employment opportunity, Weise can understand why these young men are attracted to pit bulls.

"If you look a certain way, if you've got on baggy jeans and a white tank top hanging down to your knees, you could be the greatest person in the world, but you'll be walking along and the police will stop you and ask where you're going," she said. "Pit bulls are the underdog and the media says everyone hates them, so they identify. The breed fights with so much heart and shows so much love, how could they not love that?"

There's also the protection factor.

"I've had guys tell me, 'We both know this, Lori... I can't carry a concealed weapon, but I can have a pit bull.'"

Weise has her own canine bodyguard in the form of Clancy, a 13 year-old, cropped-ear black male pit bull that a friend found passed out in her yard, starving and suffering from fight wounds, nearly two years ago.

Reactions to Clancy range from outright fear to sadness to admiration, depending on where Weise takes the dog. In the areas served by Downtown Dog Rescue, it's given Weise a certain form of respectability.

"Kids will come up and ask me, with their eyes lit up, 'Hey, do you know you have a game dog? How many fights did he win?' At first, they're so amazed, they're looking at me like I'm a martian, then all of a sudden, they start listening to me. It's like I have authority when they find out I own Clancy," Weise said.

These teachable moments are too good to pass up. Weise will explain that Clancy was indeed fought, then turned out and dumped on the street, with no food, water or place to stay. That because he never had a true home, Clancy just walked in circles until one day he broke down on her friend's yard. That Clancy had no teeth because someone had broken them all out of his mouth. When she sees tears, Weise knows she has connected on a tangible level that no amount of educational flyers will ever touch.

Money also talks. Weise is gearing up to promote The Humane Society's Stop Dogfighting campaign in Los Angeles, which offers a $5,000 reward for tips that lead to dog fighting convictions; tipsters remain anonymous. Vick is the campaign's spokesperson and if he ever makes it to Downtown Dog Rescue, Weise said she will be the first one in line to shake his hand.

"He's helped the dogs and he's helped me. I agree with my guys, Vick has done his time. I don't really know what he says behind closed doors, but all he needs to say in public is 'I'm sorry, it was wrong, and I wouldn't do this again," she said. "I'm like a dog, I'm never gonna forget, but I will forgive. Ultimately God will judge him."

***

Weather, like one's health, is often taken for granted until it's not going your way. The 320-mile drive to Baltimore was marked by rain and we didn't get to the hotel until after 5 p.m. We checked in but our room wasn't quite ready, so we sat in the truck and checked email as the rain pounded against our windshield. I looked at the back seat and patted Loren's booty. "You're a good friend for putting up with this," I told her. She looked back at me serenely and put her front paw in the air so I could rub her belly, too.

We went closer to downtown so I could get to a meeting, not just to stay sober but for my sanity. I needed human contact. Of course, I forgot to write down the exact address, so we got lost and blew a half hour. Along the way, we got to view some very cool Baltimore architecture, rows of red brick townhomes with long, vertical concrete porches, built with absolutely no space between them, and incredible churches that must date back hundreds of years.

It felt good to connect at the meeting, even though Loren set off the alarm twice, which seemed to ring especially loud through the basement walls. Still, I felt I owed Divalicious my company after her patience, so I picked up takeout at the Chicken N Trout instead of eating in at a restaurant. The name intrigued me as did the customers; the woman ahead of me had a plastic Wal-Mart bag around her coiffure.

I got an order of wings, mac n' cheese, and collard greens. The chicken was KFC-level, not bad, but not great, but the mac n' cheese was rich and satisfying and the collard greens the real deal, finished off with bits of bacon and a hint of Cajun spice. Talk about fattening, though. I consoled myself with the fact that I'd had Grape Nuts and a peach for breakfast, and vowed to eat a salad along with the crab cakes I heard one *had* to have when in Baltimore the next day.

In the morning, we slept in while waiting for the sun to come out. No luck. The endless rain didn't stop my crab cake quest, though. After consulting Yelp, I decided on SoBo Café on Cross Street and we headed downtown around 12:30. SoBo Café is nondescript on the outside, but inside it's funky and inviting, with blue and white walls, a handwritten specials board, hardwood floors, and eclectic music, from reggae to rap, playing overhead. I took a window seat and watched as a man with shoes and no socks washed another man's car in the rain.

When I saw the lunch menu, my heart sank. No crab cakes!

"I drove all the way from California to have a Baltimore crab cake and heard that yours are the best. Any way you could make an exception?" I asked the waiter.

He consulted the owner, Brent, who came over to my table.

"Yeah, I can do a crab cake for you. Usually it's $21 at dinner, how about $13?" he said.

I nodded appreciatively. I would've happily paid dinner price, I just wanted a crab cake.

"You want a big salad with that?"

The man was reading my mind.

Ten minutes later, a plate was laid before me. I bit into the softest white roll imaginable and nearly cried in delight. The crab cake wasn't cake, it was almost all lump crabmeat, sweet, tender, juicy, briny, held together with the barest of breadcrumbs and lightly fried in butter for a lusciously crisp salty tang. I added the homemade tartar sauce with capers and sank my teeth into the best meal I'd had on the trip. The salad was incredible, too, a mix of fresh baby greens with a savory homemade feta vinaigrette.

I thanked Brent and the waiter profusely and walked back to the truck, wishing I knew how to whistle because I was that happy. Loren was sitting up straight in the front seat, watching the crowds go by.

"I wish you were human sometimes, Loren, so you could have eaten that with me," I told my faithful companion. She licked my nose and I giggled.

Since it had stopped raining and we were close to the harbor, we found a parking spot and went for a walk. The Baltimore Harbor looks a bit like I would imagine Sydney, Australia does, just in smaller scale: glimmering high rises, shiny yachts, historical ships at the ready for tourists, brightly painted shops and restaurants.

"Pit bull? Where?"

That day, there were many field trips happening simultaneously, so it was a bit tough to cut through the crowds, especially when some of the kids were yelling, "Pit bull!" with a mixture of fear and excitement as they spotted us.

We walked along the river for about 20 minutes, until the sprinkles started and we made a mad dash back to the car. I was so full, all I had for dinner was a Wendy's baked potato and a peach for dessert. On the 11 o' clock news, the anchor announced that Baltimore was no longer America's deadliest city. It had moved to second place. Comforting information when it's just you and a dog in a strange motel room.

That's the weird thing about most big cities. You know that there's poverty and addiction and crime all around; you can see it in the eyes of the people and feel it in the air. But it's patchy. One minute you're driving along the projects, locking your doors, and the next, you're in high-roller territory, with McMansions lining the streets.

On our way to Philly the next morning, after I went to a Baltimore 7-11 where a sign read "Please remove your hoods," we took a detour through a suburban area rife with brick houses and endless lawns. Out of nowhere, there were dozens of Orthodox Jewish families walking on the street, pushing baby strollers, kids in tow, the men and boys in suits and hats. One man was wearing a massive furry Russian-looking thing like Fred Flintstone's "Grand Poobah" hat. The women had on plain black dresses, with simple, barrette-held long hair. Where did they come from? Where were they going?

Gidget took us straight to Pat's "King of Steaks" in Philly, where, miraculously, I scored a killer parking spot right across the street. It was exciting, like I had reached some sort of culinary Mecca. I had seen and read about Pat's for years and their cheese steak was on my list of must-try regional food items. Throngs of people were eating at tables and standing over a stainless metal counter, tilting their head sideways and attacking their thick sandwiches like pros.

Having studied in advance, I ordered my cheese steak like a local, I hoped, asking for a with and whiz, which is a pepper steak with onions and Cheese Whiz. Within 20 seconds, it was waiting for me.

"That's mine?" I asked the no-nonsense cashier.

"Yeah," he said a bit impatiently, with a gruff East Coast accent.

"Really?" I said. "So fast!"

"Yeah," he said again. I imagined his full reply would be, "Yeah, you stupid tourist, take your sandwich and move on. You're holding up the line." If only he had the time. There were at least a dozen more customers standing behind me.

The first few bites were amazing; cheesy, oily, salty, juicy, beefy goodness melding into the pillow-y white roll. The problem was, the cheese didn't trickle down to the bottom, so some bites were just beef, and when that was the case, the sandwich was, I'm sorry to say, mediocre. I've had better at Philly's Best in Saugus, a few miles from where I work. I picked out the onions and wrapped up the plain beef in a napkin for Loren.

While standing at the counter, I did meet a nice man and his daughter from Canada. He'd lived in Philly for 10 years and told me while it's safe during the day, he wouldn't go out at night.

"They've killed eight cops here in the last year," he said in disbelief.

Maybe it was Philly that was the deadliest city?

No worries. We weren't staying downtown, we were in the 'burbs by one of the largest malls in America. Fortunately, I am not a shopper, so this was not alluring to me. We drove by the Liberty Bell on our way to the hotel, but it was packed with tourists. I planned to head out first thing in the a.m. to try to beat the crowds.

Instead, we ventured over to Valley Forge National Historical Park, which allows leashed dogs throughout its massive acreage. While we couldn't go inside the Visitor's Center, which shows an 18-minute film every half hour, we could wander the many trails. The diva was excited at first, as she always is, to explore new territory. However, her stamina was not very good. It was a nice day, not too hot, but Loren was panting before we passed the half-mile mark.

I spied a cannon in the distance, so we trudged over there for a photo opp and water break. I imagined what it would be like to have fought on this land, with those crude weapons, and really couldn't fathom it.

War is bad enough nowadays, with all its clinical, high-tech weaponry. Back then, it was practically hand to hand combat. Not as gnarly as *Braveheart*, but still…it must have been horrifying.

We came across another cannon and a young couple in the distance, who were tending to a sick bird they had found. My kind of people.

"Time for a love break."

I asked the man to take our picture and he did so happily. After the shot, Loren flirted shamelessly with Brendan until he submitted to her hugs and kisses, which didn't take long.

Across the way, there were several encampment houses. Small, dank, smelling of cedar and dirt, there were bunk beds and minimal amenities. They were replicated huts, as the originals were torn down by the British in 1777, but they made the point. It was a no-frills kind of place.

Since Loren was plopping down for a break almost any chance that she got, I decided to cut the tour short and go back to the car. We took an off-path grass trail and when Loren stopped, I did, too, taking a moment to appreciate the almost angelic clouds and gorgeous blue sky overhead. "Hallelujah" rang through my head.

A little air conditioning and a lot of water put Loren back in form. We drove to the National Memorial Arch, dedicated in 1917 to the "patience and fidelity" of the soldiers who wintered at Valley Forge. Indeed. Considering what they endured, I had no right to whine about the occasional inconvenience on my cross-country road trip.

New York State of Mind

You know those shirts with "I ♥ New York?" They should make one with "I ☹ New York," just for me.

This place was insane! Besides the $20 worth of tolls it took to get there from Philadelphia and the never-ending $8 Holland Tunnel and the rude drivers and impenetrable throngs of people, there was absolutely no grass in this city! Where was a girl like Loren to do her business?

Before actually arriving in Manhattan, I got all teary-eyed when we saw the skyline from the highway. It seemed so impossible that we would make it here, all the way from California, but mile by mile we did it. I had to admit, there was something magnificent about those skyscrapers poking their way heavenward, a sense of promise and excitement that had touched millions of immigrants and Americans alike.

After going through the Holland Tunnel, we made some twists and turns and were quickly on Broadway and into the thick of things. The streets were teeming with people, of every shape, size, and nationality, coming from every direction. Never had I seen such crowds, not at a U2 concert at Dodger Stadium, not at Santa Monica Beach on the most perfect day, not at the anti-Iraq war protest in downtown Los Angeles. This was a different entity altogether.

Then there was the driving. We made our way through traffic that didn't obey signals or a sense of order. Flashes of yellow came from all four corners, honking, pushing, squeezing into impossibly tight spots, cutting me off. I quickly realized it was kill or be killed and so, fortified by a Venti green tea and lemonade, I jumped into this real-life game of Frogger with an intensity that surprised me. Soon, I was honking, cussing and acting like a native.

"You call this a parking lot?"

Our destination was Happy Paws Pet Resort, which thank God had its own parking "lot," a strip of asphalt the size of most residential driveways in Southern California. At least I didn't have to find a spot on the street. Inside, Happy Paws Pet Resort was a pleasant surprise, a two-story oasis with hardwood floors, aisles of pet supplies, and a friendly staff.

Loren was greeted by a quartet of volunteers from Animal Alliance NYC, who were holding a microchip clinic at the store. The group is part of the Mayor's Alliance for NYC's Animals, a non-profit, public-private partnership of over 160 animal rescue groups and shelters working with the City of New York toward the day when "no New York City dog or cat of reasonable health and temperament is killed merely because he or she does not have a home." Founded in 2002, the organization estimates that New York City is on track to become a no-kill community by 2015.

Animal Alliance NYC volunteers and siblings Barbara and Shawn Tolan and their father, Tim, were anticipating our visit, as was Daniel Rivera, a vet tech. All are pit bull lovers and owners.

"I think I love you, Daniel..."

"People contact me all the time about neglect situations. My sister's neighbor had a pit bull puppy that they were threatening to throw out in the streets when they moved," Daniel said. "I asked them to bring her to me instead. I could tell she'd been abused, she was hand shy and got scared over loud noises. I've had her ever since."

The dog was now a year old, a red-nosed pit named Ginger who is clearly the apple of her daddy's eye, if the way he treated Loren was any indication. In seconds flat, Loren was sitting in Daniel's lap, belly exposed, getting kisses and rubs at the same time, a look of nirvana on her face.

Loren was then led away for a grooming session with Lisa, a kind-hearted San Diego expatriate who bathed her for free because she was a California rescue dog. Lisa told me I had two or three hours to spend on my own while she took care of Loren, so I took to Broadway, home of Bloomingdales and Dean and Deluca.

I shopped like a girly girl, which is very unusual for me. My wardrobe is generally a combination of thrift store, Target, and Kohl's and my key criteria is comfort. On Broadway, I picked up a pair of dark Levis, two shirts, a strappy pair of Kenneth Cole heels, and a pair of long, dangly silver earrings for $100. Proud of my bargains and hungry, I stopped to try an authentic New York City sidewalk hot dog. The boiled frank was requisitely juicy, the bun soft and fresh, but the cart didn't offer chili...or cheese...so I got mustard and sauerkraut instead. Kind of blah, really.

The action on the streets was anything but boring, with small dramas playing out among the masses. At a stoplight, a tall, gorgeous brunette couple made out in front of me, the man even prettier than the woman, while on the sidelines, an elderly man searched the trash bins for food, his tongue sticking out. Models and madmen, mixed in with moms who pushed strollers in high heels.

Though Loren had a hard time parting with her new friends at Happy Paws, I was ready to check into The Novotel, which was quite a few blocks away. After nearly crashing into a Hyundai while parallel parking and waiting for what seemed like forever as a family from North Carolina unloaded at least a month's worth of gear, we made it to the hotel's front entrance so I could take out our bags.

"That's a good-looking dog," our doorman, a handsome older Italian, said when he saw Loren.

"Thank you," I said.

"I had a dog that looked just like her, but he passed away," he said. "His name was Stallion because he was a magnificent animal. There will never be another like him."

Loren managed the Novotel's revolving doors and elevators as if she'd been doing it all her life, then made herself right at home on the cool marble floor when we checked in. Two guys called to her from the bar and she would've gone to have a drink with them, had I let her, the hussy.

The doorman became our fast friend, directing me to the parking lot across the street where I had to leave my car (at $40 per day), as well as some places to take Loren for potty breaks. We set off over the uneven sidewalks and through the bustling restaurant patios, weaving in and out of hand-holding couples, gay and straight, cell-phone gabbers, and the million other people who all seemed to be in an incredible hurry.

For a country girl, Loren took to the city with a fair amount of ease - stopping at lights (unlike the rest of the masses) and avoiding the metal grates whenever possible. I, however, was not faring so well. No one smiled or even looked our way. Never had I felt so alone in a crowd.

Apparently, New Yorkers considered planters as parks. My kind door-man and two others directed me to streets with nothing resembling lawns, just little patches of dirt with a few vines, some were even fenced! WTF? After two miles of vain searching for grass of any kind, I stopped and started to cry.

I hated this place. I wanted to go home. I wanted my boyfriend, my dogs, and people that would smile when they saw me. I wanted to be on my hiking trail in the mountains, with nothing but the sounds of nature to soothe me, silly little Buster trotting free at my side. I wondered why the hell I was here in the first place.

I took a deep breath and composed myself. Loren was waiting patiently by my side, panting from all the exercise and, I'm sure, the manic energy that surrounded us both. We went back to the hotel and asked our doorman how to get to Central Park, which was 12 blocks away. Once there, I marveled at the incredible expanse of green and the thousands of people milling about, jogging, sleeping on park benches, playing with their own dogs. It became our regular potty stop, at least three times a day.

When we got back to our room, a bright clean space on the 26th floor facing Times Square, there was an email from Nancy at the Brittany Foundation with the headline "Good News!" I sensed immediately what it was. Loren had found a home.

Sure enough, I clicked on the email and Nancy said she had received an application on Loren from a retired widow named Cindy who had experience with big dogs as a former Rottweiler and lab/pit mix owner. A meeting and home check were scheduled, and Nancy, who can be pretty pessimistic at times, said she "felt good about it."

I collapsed on the bed and sobbed tears of sadness and joy. Loren jumped up to investigate, excitement and concern apparent in her amber eyes and furrowed brow.

"Loren, you have a home, girl," I said holding her close. "You have a home!" We snuggled for a few minutes before I faced Loren and kissed her on her pink nose. Cindy was a lucky lady to get my sweet friend to call her own, but I had Loren for almost another month and planned to make the most of it.

We celebrated Loren's adoption with room service, enjoying the night-time view of Times Square from our lofty vantage point. Lights blazed, billboards beckoned, and millions of human ants scurried about underfoot as we watched The Tony Awards on TV. They were taking place live right down the street.

***

The next day, we met with Jennifer Bristol at Animal Haven, a no-kill rescue in SoHo, for a press event arranged by Steve Gruber, director of Mayor's Alliance for Animals and their publicity firm.

Encased in warm wood, Animal Haven's storefront was both elegant and inviting. Tiny kittens played in the window display, which rapidly caught Loren's attention. She sat and cocked her head, her floppy ears erect, curious about the strange fuzzy creatures swatting at toys and scurrying up carpet trees, before I took her inside.

The shelter had a loft-like feel, three stories in all, with dogs and cats housed on each floor. The dogs got walked four times a day by a roster of volunteers and are also trained by in-house staff. On that day, Animal Haven had 19 dogs, including two litters of adorable lab and mixed breed puppies, as well as 20 cats. A beautiful female Aussie mix looked up at me from her basement kennel with one blue and one brown eye.

"She's going home tomorrow with her new family," Jennifer said proudly.

Animal Haven has a high adoption rate, including the pit bulls they take in from city shelters and owner surrenders. They also have a store that carries animal food, toys, and bedding, and the staff encourages customers to bring their small dogs in for playtime.

"It's a way to get the community involved in rescue without beating them over the head," Jennifer said. "I bought dogs 15 years ago. I didn't know that there was another way. People come in here and say, 'I didn't know I could get a Maltese or a Pug through shelters!'"

Though no press showed up for the event, Loren got plenty of attention from Gruber and Carrie Hyman, a publicist for Silver Public Relations who had arranged the event. "Oh, she's so sweet," Carrie said with her deep New York accent. "I wish I could take her home with me, but I live in a little apartment and I'm never home."

I loved hearing Carrie talk. She was in her mid-20's, with long, shiny brown hair and could have easily played a guest character on *Sex and the City*. "Yeah, she's probably not the dog for you," I said. "But I'm sure when you're ready, you'll find the right one."

"Will the paparazzi never stop?"

Carrie, Steve, Loren and I found a dog-friendly cab to take us back to Central Park. Carrie, in her wraparound sunglasses and expensive, chic clothing, fussed over Loren all the way home. The pit bull and the publicist made quite a pair.

***

I spoke too soon. I didn't hate New York. Just New York City.

We were ushered out of the city by an ominous thunderstorm as we returned from our Central Park morning walk. What started as a light drizzle under gray skies turned into big, wet splotches that stuck to my glasses and obscured my vision. I remembered when I was a kid, Elton John would perform in outlandish costumes, including glasses that had windshield wipers on them. A pair of those would have come in handy.

Everyone scurried about under umbrellas as Loren and I ran back to our hotel umbrella-less. "I haven't seen it turn black like this in years," I heard a man say as we tried not to slip on the wet streets.

Both soaked to the bone, we walked through the elegant lobby of the Novotel with as much dignity as possible amongst the well-dressed, affluent crowd. In our room, I toweled Loren off tenderly and tried to laugh it off. She rolled on her back and let me dry her midriff.

"We're getting the hell out of here, girlfriend," I told her, stroking her damp belly. "Back to the country, where we belong."

Though the parking garage was 1,000 or so linear feet from the hotel, it still took us 25 minutes to get through the traffic and back to the Novotel to collect our luggage. It felt good to be back in my truck, though. You can take the girl out of California, but you can't take California out of the girl.

Longing for some green, it was a thrill to drive out of the congestion and into the lush, open landscape surrounding the Hudson River. I thought of the U.S. Airways Flight 1549 that landed there that January. It must have been quite a ride for the passengers and the crew. Watching over the Hudson River, another page of history sprang to life before my eyes.

Tragedy by the BeeGees came on the radio and I sang along with the high-pitched parts, enough to make anyone's hair stand on end. Loren barely gave me a second glance. She was sitting up front with me, instead of snoring away in the back, out of petting reach. I laid my hand on her back and smiled, settling in for the day's journey.

Our first stop was to meet Christelle DePrete, a Best Friends writer, for lunch in West Hartford, Connecticut, a two-hour drive that took us through an upscale side of the state. The dense foliage and classically beautifully New England-style homes, set on many acres of rolling lawn, took my breath away.

Christelle was waiting for us in the parking lot and gave me a big hug. She knew what we'd been through in NYC from our blog. We settled on the patio and Christelle watched Loren so I could get my food. When I got back, Loren had her arms wrapped around Christelle's knees.

"So, why did you pick Loren out of all the dogs at Brittany to bring with you?" she asked me.

It was strange being the subject rather than the interviewer.

"She's just such a sweetheart," I told Christelle. "I had a feeling she really loved people and would be well-behaved and want to snuggle up with me at night." Boy, was I right. "My second choice was Buffy, a big, black Lab and pit mix. She's just about as sweet as Loren and has lived at the sanctuary practically her whole life. Still, Loren was always my first choice."

"Loren is a very sweet dog," Christelle said, patting Loren on the head. "This is the first pit bull I've really had any interaction with."

Suddenly, Loren was straining on her leash and whining. She had spotted a squirrel, the first of many during our lunch. Once the squirrels were out of the picture, she settled down and laid by our feet.

Christelle and I talked about the trip and her involvement with East Coast Dachsund rescue. She had a 16-year old Dachsund named Simon, whom she adopted at eight years old. "It took him a while to adjust because he was a puppy mill survivor, but once he did, he was a very happy dog," Christelle said.

Two hours went by very quickly. This tends to happen when animal welfare people come together, there's never a shortage of conversation. We bid Christelle goodbye and went on our way to Amenia, New York, to meet the women of Animal Farm Foundation, a 400-acre pit bull rescue and training center that had invited us to stay for a few nights. The non-profit's mission is to restore the image of the American Pit Bull Terrier and to protect them from discrimination and cruelty.

Crossing into New York from Connecticut, I was struck by the beauty of this part of the state. Signs dotted the road, announcing that some areas had been established in the 1700s. The pastoral scenery was spectacular, especially when we pulled up to the Animal Farm Foundation. The picturesque property boasted a massive red and white main residence, with several smaller houses and barn structures placed throughout the acreage.

I started pulling up to the main house when my cell phone rang. It was Stacey Coleman, AFF's manager.

"Am I going the wrong way?" I laughed.

"Yes, you need to turn around and head the opposite way. We'll be waiting for you," Stacey said. I could hear the smile in her voice.

Three women were standing outside a grey, two-story apartment, waving us down. We got out of the truck and Stacey engulfed me in a big bear hug before reaching down and welcoming Loren with equal affection. We were going to like it here.

Stacey, Courtney Steller, kennel manager and trainer, and Caitlin Quinn, assistant, fussed over Loren before showing us to our apartment, located under another AFF employee's house. It had a separate room with a doggy door and kennel for Loren, plus a bedroom for us both to share, bathroom, small kitchen, and laundry facilities. Heaven.

"Do you want to go on a tour or settle in? We're having dinner at my house around 6:30," Stacey said.

I opted to settle in as Courtney offered to feed Loren. She did it in a unique way, though, stuffing the wet and dry mixture into a series of Kong rubber toys. "We like to make our dogs work for their food," Courtney said. She used to be a dolphin trainer and had been at AFF since the previous October. "This is a great enrichment technique for dogs who spend time in kennels."

Wow. I'm going to have to bring this back to Brittany, I thought. Pam, the kennel worker there, was always looking for ways to keep the dogs entertained. It was just one of many tips I was to learn over the next 48 hours.

Courtney drove the heavily wooded two-lane road to Stacey's house, located about 10 minutes away from the AFF property. She is the proud mother of Brisby, a handsome rescued brindle pit mix; his Christmas photo was posted next to her SUV's speedometer.

Stacey's house was a charming, wood-sided two-story that smelled delicious when we entered. She was making lasagna and garlic bread and my mouth watered at the prospect of a home-cooked meal.

One by one, Stacey introduced me to her pack of six dogs. Gertie came first. "She hopped in my car eight years ago and changed my life," Stacey said.

At the time, Stacey was working in Indianapolis. At lunch one day, a co-worker was terrified to find a dog chasing after the fast-food sack in his hand. Stacey called the dog over and it promptly jumped into her car. The dog was a one-year old female pit bull, suffering from mange. With hardly any fur to protect her, Gertie, as she came to be known, was bleeding from her skin, which was covered in sores.

"I had two dogs and couldn't possibly take her home," Stacey said, rolling her eyes. "So I took her to the Humane Society and told them to treat her for whatever she needed. I would pay for it and help find her a home."

The humane society refused, slating Gertie for euthanasia and letting her suffer untreated in a kennel. Why? Because she was a pit bull and therefore unsuitable for adoption.

"One kennel worker tried rubbing bacon grease on her to ease her suffering, because that's what his father had taught him to do," she said. "He was the only one who attempted to help."

When she decided to adopt Gertie, Stacey was told by the shelter that she couldn't because she had lost all rights when surrendering the dog. That's when Stacey brought in a lawyer. One week later, she was the proud owner of her first pit bull, after signing extensive paperwork releasing the shelter from any liability.

Gertie has proven to be the soft touch in Stacey's pack, nursing foster kittens back to health and often acting as peacemaker for the rest of her dogs, including Franklin, a high-strung but very sweet Schnauzer.

"We call him the trailer park Schnauzer, because we don't know what he's mixed with," Stacey said.

Then there was Rudy, a black lab mix, and Josephine, a golden shepherd mix who inadvertently bit a piece off Stacey's pinky finger when she had to break up a dog fight. Oggy, a sweet little fluffy dog, constantly hugged your legs for attention, while Petunia, a fawn and white pit bull, shared a separate space in the house with one of Stacey's five cats.

"The other dogs pick on her," Stacey said. "But Petunia and the cat get along great."

Six dogs, including two pits, living in a house with five cats? How did she manage that?

"The cats know they run the house. I never let the dogs get too aggressive or assertive with them, otherwise it would never work," she said.

At bedtime, the dogs settle in with Stacey and her husband Mike in their room, all of them on the floor in dog beds except for Oggy, who scored a spot with the humans. The cats had free rein.

After the delicious meal, including hot coffeecake for dessert, Courtney drove me back to the apartment, where, outside, I met Rich, who shared the upstairs with Ashley, his girlfriend and an AFF trainer. There was a beefy, glistening, warty frog near the entrance to our temporary apartment.

"He comes here every night," Rich said.

I shuddered and grimaced.Ugh. My reptile revulsion crosses over to amphibians, so I inched my way around the creature, praying not to come into contact with its slimy skin.

Loren was laying down, content in her dog room, having eaten half of the food out of the Kongs. While I got ready for sleep, she ran to and fro, in and out of the doggy door, which she guarded until I called her in the bedroom. She immediately jumped on the twin bed, giving me approximately one-third of it to sleep on throughout the night.

I stroked her wrinkled forehead, making out the red and white markings in the twilight. She and I sighed at the same time. "I love you, boogie," I said softly and thought of how much I was going to miss her when the trip was finished. We snuggled tight and soon were fast asleep.

The next morning, Loren and I took a half-hour walk through the property, watching a line of geese make their way into a shimmering pond to join up with the other birds gracefully skating across the water. I admired the rolling hills, the wide skies, the peace of it all.

At 9 a.m., I met Stacey and Caitlin at the office/training facility, which doubles as a house for a couple of dogs. Most of the dogs here have their own room with a bed, toys and a doggy door that leads to a large, fenced enclosure.

Benson, a fawn and white male, just one year old, was out and about when I came in. A shelter rescue with long, pointy ears, Benson roamed the office area excitedly, tearing into a squeaky, thrashing it about like a shark, stopping only for occasional affection breaks.

Ashley took Benson into the training room and worked with him on a technique called shaping, which she explained was providing an object for a dog to touch without pointing to it, then giving treats and positive reinforcement when he or she got anywhere near it. Eventually, the dog figured out the main objective. "Shaping requires them to think more. It's a really good mental exercise," Ashley said.

Within minutes, Benson was following Ashley's suggestion of touching her right and left palms with his nose. Every time he did, she'd make a noise with her clicker and give him a treat. Each treat had a value. Low was kibble, medium was a chunk of dog food roll, and high was something really pungent, like dried liver, salmon, or beef. The stinkier the better.

Punky, a brown and white charmer, was next. This little girl could actually jump rope, skipping in and out of the moving line as Ashley made her commands, while I shook my head in awe. Training time over, we delivered Punky back to her room, which was decorated in a cheerful Hawaiian theme in a standalone building with a large yard outside the kennel. It even had a custom pit painting by Beth, an AFF employee, above her futon. Pretty stylish digs.

Courtney then took us to "downtown," which was a more traditional kennel setting, with wire enclosures inside and a place to potty outside. "Some dogs are actually calmer in a kennel where they can see other dogs and have more stimulus," she explained.

Scarface was one such resident, a snow-white one-year-old male with a serious bulldog underbite and a lot of character. We petted him through the gate.

Overall, Animal Farm Foundation has about 20 dogs at any given time, mostly pulled from NYC shelters. These are some very lucky pit bulls, as AFF not only has awesome accommodations, they spend every day training, socializing, and exercising the dogs.

"We don't subscribe to the myth that every pit bull is dog aggressive," Stacey said. "Many of our dogs enjoy play dates together and can be housed with other dogs, should potential adopters already have one."

Since we had plans to go into the city for an art exhibit and were leaving at 2:30 p.m., Ashley and Stacey had me get Loren for a brief training session in the office area. She responded very well to the clicker and was soon laying down on command.

Outfitted with a clicker and treat-filled pouch, at Ashley's instruction, I had Loren sitting and stopping to make eye contact with me in short order. It was shocking how easy it was, requiring only patience and time.

"This is a great technique for when you're walking and she gets excited about another dog or distracted by something," Ashley said. "You can have her make eye contact with you and get refocused."

"What if you only have time to do this for a few minutes, three or four days a week?" I asked, thinking of the Brittany dogs and how beneficial this could possibly be for them.

"Any time you spend doing this for the dogs is good for them. It not only helps make them more adoptable, the mental stimulation is tiring for them, which is helpful when they spend a lot of time in a kennel," Ashley said.

Back at our apartment, I switched from my standard uniform of jeans, tennis shoes, and a hoodie to new dark jeans, the Kenneth Cole sandals, and a black sweater, topped with my $5 Pashmina knockoff, for our trip to NYC. Bernice Clifford, the lead behaviorist at AFF, drove me, Caitlin, and Stacey in Stacey's SUV, bringing along her GPS, Sally. (Everyone seems to name their GPS; my parents' is Barbie.)

We were off to attend *Dutch Seen: New York Rediscovered,* an exhibit of contemporary Dutch photographers at the Museum of the City of New York. Charlotte Dumas, one of the artists, had photographed several NYC shelter pit bulls, including an AFF rescue named Gretel.

First, we had dinner at Hanratty's, a leather and wood-clad neighborhood joint that has been in business since 1917, and looked it. I had the Cajun chicken and pasta with broccoli rabe, not finishing much after scarfing down too many hot, fresh rolls with butter. The rest of the table went vegetarian. Not surprisingly, many animal welfare workers and volunteers don't eat meat.

"What has been the most surprising thing for you about AFF?" Stacey asked me.

I paused for a moment. "I knew it was going to be amazing, but I'm just so impressed with how much time and effort you spend on each dog," I said. "I didn't realize the training was going to be so extensive."

I thought again.

"That and how nice the facilities are for each dog. They have it better than a lot of people," I said.

They laughed.

We had our leftover pasta wrapped up so we could try to find a homeless person to give it to. Stacey and I were on the lookout as we made our way back to the museum. She revealed that she used to help refugees from other countries find housing and work when she lived in Indianapolis, including a Pakistani woman and her five children. Stacey took in the latter personally when the mom fell ill and was hospitalized.

"For how long?" I asked.

"Oh, about three weeks," she said.

"That's a long time!"

Stacey shrugged.

"Wow," I said, impressed. "You're a chronic philanthropist, huh? I mean, a chronic do-gooder..."

"When I see wrong in the world, I just can't sit back and accept it. I have to do what I can to change it," Stacey replied.

We left our pasta on a park bench, having found no candidates along the route. Inside the museum, the rich, the powerful, and the beautiful were mingling in a sea of Chardonnay and designer labels. Tall blondes with amazing bone structure abounded, as the audience was largely Nordic.

Dumas exhibit

I put my camera around my neck and observed through the lens, always more comfortable in the worker bee role than making any attempt to be social, especially in this upscale crowd.

The photographs ranged from the whimsical to the sad to the serious. Dumas' dog portraits were very commanding, illustrating the tough lives these dogs led in a single snapshot, many of them scarred, a harrowed look in their eyes.

Stacey, Bernice, and Caitlin were all very proud of the Gretel portrait, which represented a Guardian Angel over the other dogs, as she had found a home and new life. The epilogue for the rest were a mystery. As we read the artist's biography and exhibit copy, the mood turned somber. In the text, referring to the dogs, was the phrase "many given up because of their aggressive nature."

"Oh, this is unacceptable," Stacey said. "I am going to get this changed." (She did, the next morning. The museum not only took her call, the employee apologized, promised to fix it, and even offered an opportunity to bring the AFF dogs up for a night. I wasn't surprised. Stacey was more fierce than the breed she loved so much.)

Bernice requested an impromptu visit to NYC Animal Care & Control shelter on our way back. She wanted to see if there were any dogs there that might be good AFF candidates. This was unexpected. I struggled on whether or not to go in. I hate shelters. It always makes me cry to see the dogs in cages, many without any hope. In the end, I decided to accompany them. I am a journalist. I had to face reality and report back my findings, whether I liked them or not.

A volunteer was walking a large brown boxer/pit mix on the street outside the shelter. I called over, "Handsome boy."

"He needs a home," the volunteer responded.

I smiled in recognition. "Wish I could take him," I replied. "Good luck, though."

We went to the adoption area, which was located at the back of the building. The first dog I saw was an older black bully with a scarred face, wagging her tail. Second dog I saw was a black and white bully. Third dog a red and white. And so on.

At least 80 percent were pits or pit mixes or dogs that look like pit bull, as AFF likes to say. A playful chocolate beauty caught Bernice's eye and she noted the dog's impound information.

Unfortunately, we weren't done yet. Bernice led the way to the intake area. While there, we saw a woman taking home a mature cat and

"Please get me out of here..."

tiny little kitten she had adopted. She was very excited about her new family members, named Ginger and Bella, and I was thrilled for all of them.

"Bless you for adopting," I told her as we headed down a gray, windowless hallway. Dogs were separated in a series of kennels for temperament evaluation, since they had to be determined eligible for adoption. Again, bully after bully, with a few fluffy shepherds or senior labs mixed in.

There was also a quarantine area for sick animals and lastly, a death row area for those scheduled to be euthanized. I only made it to the third door down, which had double decker kennels. An old black cocker spaniel was on top of a pit bull. I knew who would be more likely to survive.

I ran back to the lobby area, where I wasn't the only one crying. A young girl, her lip pierced, was holding a stuffed Rottweiler, silent tears running down her face as her mother and boyfriend brought in a trash-bag wrapped dog. They were there to have their Rottweiler cremated.

A blonde female volunteer came over to me, bending down to look me in the eye.

"Are you OK?"

"No, I'm not," I replied. "I just hate this."

She nodded in sympathy.

"We are a horrible species," I said. "Humans are a horrible species to let this happen."

"I know," the volunteer said. Her name was Megan. "I know."

I sighed and looked into her empathetic blue eyes. "I really admire you for what you do here, though. I volunteer at a no-kill shelter because I can't handle this."

"Yeah, it can be really hard," Megan said. "I'm signing up for the compassion program, but I'm not sure if I'm going to be able to do it or not."

Megan went on to explain that the compassion program is for the euthanasia-scheduled dogs. They get to go for an extra walk, have a nice dinner, sleep on a warm blanket, and be doted on by volunteers before they are killed.

I sobbed harder. What a beautiful and ugly thing.

She also told me about the "Safety Net" program, aimed toward helping public housing tenants of New York City Housing Authority who had recently been ordered to turn in their over-25 pound dogs. Some residents felt it was just a cover to rid the area of pit bulls without instituting an actual breed ban and were trying everything they could to fight it.

According to Megan, other owners were turning over their large dogs, primarily pit bulls, to the shelter in droves.

"I have a lady who has two pits she's desperately trying to keep. I told her I'll do everything I can to help her," Megan said. "We can often put dog owners in touch with legal resources and avoid them having to turn in their pet."

Our conversation was interrupted by a massive, golden pit bull mix dragging a cop into the lobby. He had a four-inch wide leather belt around his neck, a makeshift leash or chain that looked like it had been snapped off at the end.

"Yeah, we found him knocking over trash cans and breaking into stores, eating Vanilla Wafers," the male cop said, struggling to manage the dog. "Poor guy. Happens all the time. People get puppies, then they don't want the responsibility, so they just dump the dogs in the streets…or they get free from their chains and run away."

I watched the golden bully be led away by shelter staff, who were very kind and genial with him. Perhaps for some dogs, a shelter is a step up. At least they have, well, shelter, food, and attention. For however long. I prayed this big, awkward boy would get a second chance with a family who would love him, one that would not treat him like a burden or a piece of trash to be disposed of.

On the way home, in the car with the AFF girls, I couldn't stop the tears from falling. "I'm sorry," I said through sniffles.

"No need to apologize here," Stacey said. "We all get it."

"What is it that's specifically bothering you?" Bernice asked gently.

"How do you choose? How do you choose who's going to live and who's going to die? How do you walk through those kennels, knowing most of those dogs won't make it out alive?" I asked.

Bernice looked out the window, pausing before she replied.

"I try to look at it from a positive perspective. This shelter has improved so much over the last few years. They used to all be double decker kennels, with no protection at the bottom and lips on the edges that would often break the dogs' legs when they were being pulled out," she said. "The staff and volunteers have changed, too. They used to be somewhat indifferent, and now it seems like they really care."

Bernice continued. "It's not just the conditions that have improved, but the adoption rates have jumped from 5 percent to about 45 percent for the pit bulls and 70 percent for overall breeds," she said.

"That's great," I acknowledged.

The car was quiet for a moment. "You can only do so much," Bernice said finally. "At least our dogs get a chance at a whole new life."

"Nighty night…"

So did Loren, thanks to the Brittany Foundation. She was pulled from a high-kill shelter, just another pit bull scheduled for death, before being rescued.

At bedtime, I gave Loren the new woobie that Stacey and the rest of girls included in a goody bag for us. She snuggled right up with it and went to sleep.

***

111

I was sad to leave AFF and I think Loren was, too. We walked around the next morning, taking in the sights and smells before I headed over to the office for breakfast.

"What's your schedule like today?" Stacey asked after I expressed my sadness.

"Nothing major. Just have to drive to Cooperstown," I said. "About 200 miles."

"Why don't you stay for our training class at 1 p.m. then?," Stacey said.

Yeah. This gave us time to get cleaned up, packed, and head to town for lunch, as well as more training lessons. We hopped in the truck and got ourselves a sandwich before class.

There were four other dogs in the training room, along with AFF staff and a married couple of scientists visiting from California. The husband, a geneticist, was working on research that would prove a dog's breed did not attest to its inherent aggressiveness, which he hoped would go a long way in preventing or overturning breed specific legislation.

Loren took her place with Courtney, who brought her in the room last. She looked around with curiosity, then a bit of nervousness for a few seconds. In no time, however, Loren was putty in Courtney's clicking, treating hands, rolling around on the floor and barely noticing the other dogs around her.

Bernice watched Loren with a practiced eye. She began training dogs after acquiring a six-month old bully from a shelter and being asked to leave obedience class because of her new dog's breed. After eight years at AFF, Bernice has helped hundreds of pit bulls and dogs who look like them acquire the successful behaviors that got them adopted.

"Loren's a really good dog," Bernice said after a few minutes. "She's solid, comfortable, confident. For a dog that's been in a shelter for two years, Loren's really incredible. She's home ready."

I smiled like a proud mama, make that auntie, then gulped and asked Bernice the questions that had been haunting me.

"Bernice, do you think I'm doing Loren more harm than good with this trip? I don't want her to think that I'm her person...only to have me take her to her new home. Do you think this will be confusing to her?" I said.

"Michelle, any time you take a shelter dog out of its environment and expose them to new situations and socialize them, it's a good thing," she replied.

"Thank you," I said, satisfied, and went back to watching Loren.

Stacey had noticed something from across the room. Bear, a handsome brown male, was flirting with Loren, making eye contact, whining, and wanting an introduction. She suggested they go for a walk together.

Ashley and Stacey walked the dogs while I followed closely with a camera. "We'll just take it slow and see if there's any interest on Loren's part," Stacey said.

Bear was raring to go, but Loren didn't seem to notice him much. She was much more fixated on the goings-on at the farm. Bear, however, was pretty firmly keen on Loren.

"Face it, Bear, I'm just not that into you."

"He so wants to sniff her butt right now," Stacey said, making us all laugh.

Ashley held Loren with strength and ease as Bear made his approach. Loren looked at him with a furrowed brow, which was a slight sign of stress. They got within a couple inches of each other, but Loren wasn't really having it. No aggression, just ruffled fur and a disinterest bordering on rude. There would be no butt sniffing today.

After getting permission from Nancy at The Brittany Foundation, Bernice drew Loren's blood for a DNA analysis. Bernice suspected Loren might be part boxer, which was something I always wondered, but the rest of the AFF girls insisted she was staffie or pit bull. In a few days, we would know for sure.

One by one, we said our goodbyes. Pulling away from the farm, I smiled through my tears. We had made great friends, but another adventure awaited. That was the beauty and curse of life on the road.

We drove to Cooperstown, where I had made camping reservations, in about four hours. The winding back roads gave me another opportunity to appreciate New York's beauty, its fertile farmlands, the charming homes spaced out amongst the acreage.

Since it was after 5 p.m., the park ranger had already left. Instructions at the gate said we could go to the cabins and check in the next day, so off we went. The place was gorgeous, dense with trees, fresh air, and rustic log cabins. This would be a perfect resting place for a few days…except there were no bathrooms in the cabins or cell service on the grounds. One maybe I could have lived with. Both were unacceptable. We hightailed it out of there and I frantically scanned Gidget for hotels in the area. Most of them were independent and probably wouldn't accept dogs.

Finally, Gidget came up with a pet-friendly chain hotel in Norwich, so we spent another hour driving to our new home. The hotel was located right off the highway, across from a dairy bar, where they serve ice cream made from local milk, and down the road from a charming Main Street/downtown area. This would do nicely.

I stopped for a little carb comfort at Pasquales, an authentic pizzeria complete with brusque waitresses, talk of the Yankees, and accents I'd only previously heard on *The Sopranos*. The restaurant was family run; the waitress called the wiry, tattooed gentleman tossing pizza "Pops" and her brother was the delivery man. I loved it. The pasta with red sauce and sausage was delish, too. We drove to the dairy bar, where I got a soft serve chocolate cone.

We sat at the outdoor bench table as the night turned dusky. Loren looked longingly at me, but I didn't think dairy was good for dogs...and I knew chocolate wasn't.

"Sorry, girl," I said, patting her on the head. "Not this time."

The next day was fairly unplanned, so I could catch up on my writing and laundry. Loren and I took a lunch break at noon, happening upon Hot Diggity Dog a few miles from the hotel, where they gave her a free frank of her own in addition to my chili cheese dog purchase. They were nice people, rescuers with a Pomeranian from a hoarding case, plus five cats, several rabbits, and fish.

***

Niagara Falls was the next destination, some five hours away and we took our time getting there, observing the small villages and towns along the countryside, where many cows resided and more than one operating tractor was spotted. For sustenance and motivation, we stopped at Dunkin Donuts for a large iced tea and donut holes. I'm not sure if America runs on Dunkin, but New York sure seems to. They are as ubiquitous here as Starbucks is in California.

The town of Niagara Falls was not as I expected. Instead of a natural wonder backdrop, it was more like a tacky Las Vegas strip, without any grand hotels to class things up. Just miles of motels, strip malls, and tourist shops. Even the entrance to the park was gaudy. Crowded, too. The parking lot attendant suggested we come back in the morning, which sounded like a much better plan.

Craving a nature fix, we stopped along the Water Fowl Viewing area overlooking the Niagara River and took a mile-long walk. We saw just one duck, skimming across the water, but that was fine. The river itself was something to behold, especially under a blanket of striated white clouds, the golden sun filtering in and reflecting on the water.

After checking into our hotel, we headed 12 miles to Buffalo, where *Roadfood* mentioned a must-try hot dog joint named Ted's. I was also on a quest for frozen custard at the behest of my editor, Michele, who insisted I try this delicacy before leaving the East Coast. Serendipitously, an Anderson's Frozen Custard stand was located right across the street from Ted's, which was hopping on a Saturday night.

Lines snaked around the tables, almost to the door. Inside, the sizzle of the grill and the tantalizing aroma got my mouth watering. I ordered a chili cheese dog, onion rings, and a loganberry juice, and took it to the table outside. The dog was topped with a satisfying layer of spicy homemade hot sauce and chili under a blanket of cheese and the onion rings were amazing, a tangled, crispy mass of fried goodness (or badness, depending on how you looked at it).

The frozen custard at Anderson's was a find, too; creamy, silky, yet somehow lighter than traditional ice cream. I lapped it up and tried to ignore Loren's baleful look from the passenger seat.

Full and tired, we returned to our hotel. After all the driving and not getting to see Niagara Falls yet, I was a bit grumpy, so I wasn't thrilled when Loren, also in a funk, decided to circle our hotel at least ten times on our nightly poop walk. She made all the motions and I knew it was time for her to go (when you spend 24/7 with anyone, you get to learn their habits), so I was growing unhappier by the second.

"Damn it, will you just poop, you diva?" I asked her. "I'm sick of this."

Loren just kept going round and round, sniffing, stopping, but no action.

Ten minutes later, I sat down on a curb, threw down the leash and started crying. I was exhausted. I missed my own dogs, whom Wayde had sent pictures of that morning. I also missed him, my friends, my mountain home. I was sick of the hotels, the checking in, the unloading and reloading, the driving, the inconvenience of it all, not knowing anyone. All of it.

Loren just looked at me, her front legs crossed, confused, her amber eyes blinking fast.

"Look at all I've done for you and you can't even poop for me? Is that too much to ask?"

More blinking.

I took a deep breath and stopped crying. I had lost it. Poor Loren. She was such a good sport about everything and here I was yelling at her like a complete freak. It wasn't her fault. She had the right to take her time and poop where she wanted.

She finally did. We went back to the room, a bit estranged. Loren stretched out on the mattress as I got ready for bed. I put my face close to hers and looked her in the eye.

"I'm sorry," I told her. "I'm an ass sometimes. I appreciate your patience with me."

She sighed and we snuggled up together. Never go to bed angry, right?

Wayde told me that seeing Niagara Falls the next day would change my attitude, so we got there early, around 9 a.m. There was a smattering of people, but nothing crazy like the day before.

We heard the rush of water before glimpsing the falls. The Niagara River, hundreds of yards under our feet, was sea-foam blue, a rainbow perched in its mist.

Around the bend, the falls pounded their way to the river below, creating several more rainbows. I took a deep breath and watched in awe. Wayde was right. There was nothing like nature to put you in your right place.

The park itself was magnificent, with its acres of manicured lawns encircled by smaller rapids and falls to admire, as well a bridge that led to the opposite side of the falls, closer to Canada, for viewing.

We spent an hour checking out everything that allowed dogs (there were some exhibits, movies, and tours that didn't).

Loren, of course, was much more enthralled with the squirrels that teased her throughout our walk than the falls. She wasn't scared of the water or the sound it made, which made me really proud. The girl could hang in pretty much any situation.

"Another natural wonder...wait, is that a squirrel?"

On our way back, I noticed several dog owners enjoying the trails, too. An elderly man sat with his black cocker spaniel, taking in the view and talking to the dog. I waved and he waved back, an unspoken camaraderie between us.

Niagara Falls was a turning point for us - literally and figuratively. We had gone as far east as our itinerary allowed and were turning back for California. I hugged Loren as we got back in the car.

"We did it, Loren, we did it," I said, nuzzling into her soft muzzle. She was panting and slobbery, with bits of foam around the corners of her mouth, but I didn't care.

"Thank you for being such a good companion. Thanks for putting up with me," I told her. "We're heading home."

Her response was an enthusiastic lick. Somehow, I suspected Loren might be ready to go west, too.

PitsBurgh

Sometimes the best things in life are unexpected. So it was with Pittsburgh, a stop that wasn't originally on the itinerary.

It all started with a woman named Rebecca Courtad, who had found our website through Facebook in May. She donated $50 and extended an invitation for us to come to the city where she lived. Rebecca volunteered with the Western Pennsylvania Humane Society and we quickly became e-mail pals.

Before the trip, I had told Rebecca that as far as Pennsylvania was concerned, we would only make it as far as Philly. "I'm bummed you can't come to Pittsburgh, but hope you have an amazing trip," she e-mailed back.

However, when Stacey Coleman at Animal Farm Foundation told me of the vicious breed ban enacted against pit bulls in much of the state of Ohio, which was our original route to head back west, I ditched our plans to see Cleveland and the Rock N' Roll Hall of Fame. The possibility of Loren being confiscated and killed, though unlikely, was too much of a risk.

I looked on the map and came up with an alternative route, which allowed us to make a stop in Pittsburgh. "Looks like we can meet after all," I wrote Rebecca excitedly.

Unfortunately for us, Rebecca was on her way to Florida for vacation. "I can't believe I'm going to miss you," she emailed me. "But there are several volunteers and staff that would love to meet with you and Loren."

One of them was Abby Kirkland and her 11-year old son, Reid, who rendezvoused with us at Rita's, a frozen custard stand in the Greentree neighborhood, a leafy suburb with cool New England architecture and narrow streets.

We had made our way to Pittsburgh from Niagara Falls and it was 240 miles of picturesque country, clear blue skies and rolling hills of green. The leisurely day allowed for a stop at Lake Erie, a massive, sparkling body of water festooned with water-skiers and sailboats. I enjoyed the scene from a local eatery's second story patio, while Loren took a snooze in the truck.

The search for a decent hotel took us into downtown Pittsburgh first, which we entered via a sturdy yellow bridge. Major cities look much the same to me: high-rises, congested roads, and too many people. Pittsburgh had some nice architecture and outdoor art installations in the mix, but still...not our scene. We headed to the suburbs and found a safe-looking Red Roof Inn before meeting with Abby and Reid.

It was Abby who introduced Loren to frozen custard. The cashier, apparently a dog lover, had given her a complimentary dish of vanilla for Loren to sample.

"Are you sure it's OK for her to eat ice cream?" I asked like a nervous first-time mother.

"Oh, it's fine," Abby reassured me. "My dogs eat it all the time."

"Mmm, more, please!"

Loren sure loved it, lapping it up like an eager kid, the custard melted and smeared around her fuzzy pink snout. She seemed very disappointed when the treat ended.

To distract her, Reid took Loren on a series of several small walks, while I got to know Abby. She's volunteered at WPHS for several years, sometimes fostering, but usually playing matchmaker for prospective adopters and the available dogs. She, like a lot of volunteers, has a soft spot for bully breeds, which make up the majority of dogs at the shelter.

"It's a tough situation," Abby sighed. "They're such great dogs."

She often brought Reid to the shelter to volunteer. He had an ease with Loren that belied his years, walking her with strength and controlling her with authority when a couple came to the same patio with a small black dog. He also fielded questions about her by curious patrons.

By the end of our date, Loren was sitting in Reid's lap. I was very impressed with him. During both of my short-lived marriages, there was a brief window where I thought I wanted children, and fantasized, ironically enough, about having a daughter named Lauren. That window quickly closed when I realized how much work was involved with being a mother and what it would do to my freedom. If one could be guaranteed to have a child as great as Reid, however, maybe I would have done it anyway. Maybe.

"What a cool kid," I told Abby. "I wish there were more like him."

Since Reid had a pressing game of Capture the Flag to attend to, they bid us goodbye and we went back to our room for a long night of watching *True Blood* on HBO. Loren stretched out across her side of the bed, taking up a good six feet, snoring contentedly, dreaming, possibly, of eating frozen custard on a hot summer day.

I decided to call her new mom, Cindy, who lived in Valencia, where I worked. Nancy had told Cindy I would be introducing myself from the road.

Her voice sounded older than I anticipated, kind of nasal, the cadence slow. I knew Cindy was retired, but she sounded downright fragile.

"What made you want to adopt Loren?" I asked her.

"Well, I don't know," Cindy replied, pausing for a moment. "She just seems so sweet."

"Loren is a sweetheart," I told her. "She is a very affectionate dog and likes a lot of attention."

"Well, that's good…since it's just me here, she'll be the only one I have to give affection to," Cindy said.

She told me that she liked to travel a little, which was perfect, and that Loren would be able to sit on the couch with her at night and watch TV, which warmed my heart. Cindy already had a dog bed and a food dish for Loren, as well as toys.

"I saw from The Signal articles that she likes her toys," she said.

"She does," I said, touched. Cindy was certainly prepared.

After I hung up with Cindy, I quickly dialed Nancy.

"Nancy, how old is Cindy? She sounds ancient!," I said.

"Well, she's in her 60s," Nancy said.

"Is she frail or something? She just sounded…weak," I said.

"No," Nancy assured me. "Cindy's in good health, solidly built. She's had big dogs before. I think she's going to be just fine." She went on to tell me about Cindy's house, which met with Nancy's strict fencing criteria, and that everything else checked out OK.

If Nancy was vouching for Cindy, then who was I to judge? An older woman just wasn't who I envisioned Loren to be with. I thought she'd be with someone younger, hipper, who would take her out on coffeehouse patios or hiking in the Hollywood Hills or for walks along the beach.

Still, I was happy for Loren. After two years in a kennel, she was finally going to a home. I'd miss her, of course, but this had been my dream all along, that Loren would find her forever person at the end of our journey. There was just a part of me that didn't feel 100 percent about Cindy.

***

We awoke early the next morning, or I should say I woke up and nudged Loren out of a deep sleep to make our appointment at Western Pennsylvania Humane Society at 9 a.m.

After a quick breakfast of yogurt and fruit in the hotel room, we headed back to the city. The day coincided with the big Penguins Stanley Cup victory parade in downtown Pittsburgh, not too far from the shelter's location, so I was anxious we might be late.

Surprisingly, we sailed over the bridge through the light traffic and made it early to the shelter, a brownstone building located in a semi-industrial part of the city. Several dogs were being walked around the neighborhood by volunteers, including a big, beautiful brindle bully.

In the lobby, a volunteer named Theresa greeted us with a friendly grin. Loren immediately introduced herself with a big sloppy kiss and forceful hug, nearly knocking poor, petite Theresa out of her wheelchair.

"I'm sorry," I said, pulling a reluctant Loren off.

"No problem," Theresa said. "I love all the dogs that come in here."

Once Loren was deposited in the executive director's office, Gretchen Fieser, the WPHS director of public relations and business relationships, gave me a tour. The facility was a large, open, two-story building painted in bright, cheerful colors, with appealing graphics and several kennel areas, as well as an adoption floor and training room.

WPHS, started in 1874, is one of America's oldest humane societies. As an "open door" shelter, they take in all types of animals...and I mean all. Goats, chickens, rabbits, gerbils, even...

"We get one or two alligators a year," Gretchen said. "The biggest one was about four feet. He lives at a sanctuary in Florida now."

Approximately 14,000 animals come through WPHS' doors annually, with 400 to 500 animals residing in the building at any given time. Adoption rates are approximately 50 percent; the rest are euthanized. All of the animals are vaccinated at intake and spayed or neutered if determined eligible for adoption. We witnessed firsthand the spaying of Shy, a beautiful fawn-colored female pit bull, at the onsite medical clinic.

Gretchen briefly introduced me from the hallway and was happy to share that Shy already had a home. "Oh, that's fantastic. It's always good to know they're being adopted, especially the pits," the vet said, her eyes grinning above her surgical mask.

Volunteers at WPHS walk the dogs every day and interact with cats to lessen kennel stress. Some get adopted right away, some can wait for weeks, even months. After 90 days in the shelter environment, dogs have been known to deteriorate mentally to the point that they are no longer adoptable and are then killed.

Cats make up the largest number of intakes. Some are feral, but many are owner-surrendered. Gretchen took me into the cat area, where teeny tiny kittens were in cages alongside more mature cats. A young black cat pawed at his crate, meowing for affection. I scratched his head and felt the tears coming. Others just looked at me, wide-eyed. Every cage was full. I shook my head and could feel the burn of anger begin at the base of my neck. How hard is it to take care of a cat, for Christ's sake?

Reasons for relinquishment varied, as Gretchen read the tags aloud. "Moving. Allergies. Kid left home and mom didn't want to take care of cat," she recited.

Next, we met the dogs who were in the intake area being eva-luated for temperament and the dogs who made it to the adoption floor.

Just like NYC, it was bully after bully after bully. Black ones, white ones, beige ones, spotted ones, brindle ones, sad ones, friendly ones, and young ones playing together, oblivious to their situation.

"Are you our new person?"

A brown and white bully with a comical under-bite and anxious eyes caught my gaze. I found his quirkiness charming and hoped someone else would, too. Holding back tears, I silently said a quick prayer for him and his kennel mate, a black and white beauty, as we continued down the floor.

There were also shepherds, beagles, Sharpeis, and the fattest yellow lab I had ever seen. "Owner got ill and couldn't take care of anymore," read his chart.

Pit bulls and pit bull mixes make up 35 to 50 percent of available dogs on the WPHS adoption floor any given day; the number sometimes drops to as low as 20 percent and climbs as high as 80 percent.

Joey, a 12-year old, crop-eared black male pit bull graying at the muz-zle, was surrendered to WPHS when his owner went to jail. Gretchen took one look at his wise face, fell in love, and brought him home that night. A gentle giant who loves kids and even kittens, Joey's new life included acting as an ambassador for WPHS educational outreach programs. He now accompanied Gretchen to public relations events, including an annual trip to educate employees at Saks Fifth Avenue.

"One woman pet Joey and said, 'He's so sweet. I just love him.' She then asked me what kind of dog he was. When I told her he was a pit bull, she yanked her hand back," Gretchen said, shaking her head in disbelief at the memory.

When Gretchen talks to teens at juvenile detention centers throughout the city, it's a no-holds barred interaction. Boys, especially, have very specific questions, as she illustrated.

"One kid jumped up and asked me, 'If a dog gets neutered does it still have a penis? When I said yes, he said 'You should've said so. So, he can still have sex?'" Gretchen recalled. "They don't like the idea of neutering. You have to change the message from one of fixing to birth control for them to buy in."

***

While Gretchen was reaching out to those behind bars, Ron Smith, a WPHS humane officer since 1971, was taking it to the streets, trying to keep order in a uncivilized world.

Concerned neighbors call WPHS every day, mostly with complaints of neglect: dogs with no shelter during the tough winters, no visible food, no medical treatment for obvious ailments. Ron, who oversees four counties, estimated seventy percent of their calls involve pit bulls or pit bull mixes.

"This has been going on for so long. When pits became popular in this area in the late 70s, early 80s, I thought it was a fad that would go away, but I don't see a different breed coming into play anytime soon," he said.

If enough cause is found from a call, Ron can issue a criminal complaint or a search warrant. Sometimes, a pet owner is doing enough to meet basic code requirements, requiring Ron to walk away from a situation he personally dislikes. Potential violators are placed on a list and inspected frequently by Ron and his colleagues, who attempt surveillance work to monitor how many animals are on a property and how frequently new dogs are taken in.

"What happens a lot is that we may go to a place, but the resident tenant is not home. We may see four or five dogs, so we'll leave a notice," he said. "When we go back, everything's gone. These are dogs that are generally tied up or left behind in vacant homes, so they'll move them to other people's properties and tie them up or put them in a shed there."

Some callers suspect that dogs are being used for fighting, their scars telltale signs. It's a common occurrence in the low-income neighborhoods that Ron patrols to find former fighting pits tied to a tree, tied to a bridge, once they've served their purpose.

"We are able to rehabilitate a few of these dogs, bring them back to a normal body weight and rehome them, but for the most part, they're so emaciated, in such poor condition, that they're near death, if not dead already, and don't make it," he said.

Other callers complain about the number of dogs in one home or a pregnant dog not being properly taken care of. Backyard breeding is a big problem in Pittsburgh, as Ron illustrated.

"These neighborhood hoodlums, as I call them, have puppies to make a quick buck. They breed their dogs every time they're in heat and try to sell the puppies," he said.

When they don't sell, oftentimes because the market is saturated, the puppies end up in shelters such as WPHS. As if to drive the point home, during my tour of the shelter, a young African American man was waiting in the lobby to surrender two four-month old pit bull mixes, disposable inventory that no longer made business sense.

Ron tries to combat the problem with education but acknowledges his primary audience is particularly tough: known drug dealers, wanted felons, and hardened gang-bangers.

"You're talking about people involved in homicides, criminal mentalities that have no concern about human or animal life," he said. "How do you reach the hearts of these people? I don't know. Incarceration doesn't seem to help. They're not afraid of anything. They just don't care."

***

WPHS intake team leader Susie Gilbert got tired of seeing pit bulls overflowing in kennels on the adoption floor: the puppies from backyard breeders and negligent owners, the full-grown dogs surrendered from neighboring areas of Ohio where they are outlawed, the never-ending parade of strays young and old.

She decided to take action.

Susie created the Super Seven program in July 2008. Designed to help pit bulls stand out from the canine crowd with intensive training and socialization, 89 Super Seven graduates were successfully placed in homes during its first year.

Super Seven candidates are tested in a number of areas using the ASPCA's "Meet Your Match" Canine-ality program as criteria for eligibility. The areas include greeting (level of sociability and arousal), left alone (house manners and energy levels), play (interest, focus and sociability), food motivation (how hard will the dog work for something it wants), manners (overall behavior and awareness), and crate (optional, but important for certain adopters).

Once they pass the Canine-ality program, Super Seven pits are trained by volunteers to do tricks such as sit, shake, lay down, and roll over, and interact with other dogs. They are also taught how to enthusiastically greet potential adopters.

"Super Seven gives the dogs that normally wouldn't get looked at more of a chance. We teach them how to behave appropriately in a kennel, so people are drawn to them, which is especially helpful if they're black or plain-looking," Susie explained.

The formula is working: Paco, a nine-year old male graduate of the Super Seven program, was recently adopted by a 67-year old retiree. Trinity, a young female, was so impressive with her training, she found a home within 24 hours.

Susie has received requests from close to a dozen shelters across the country, asking for information on how to start a "Super Seven" in their community, which she was more than happy to share.

According to Susie, giving pit bulls the skills to make a good impression is vital to combating their negative media image; in Pittsburgh, pit bull attacks and bites are relentlessly reported, while other breeds' misdeeds are kept quiet.

"We get Golden Retrievers and Labradors turned in to WPHS because they've mauled the family child, but you never hear about that," she said. "The sensationalism with pit bulls just kills us. Because of how they're labeled in the news, whether they're a true pit bull or a mix, a lot of people don't want to adopt one, especially as a family dog."

Susie, a stocky brunette with a no-nonsense East Coast demeanor, admitted to a particular fondness for the breed. "They're the underdogs. I always pick the underdogs," she said. "They remind me of me. They have a rough, tough exterior, but once you get to know them, they're real softies."

Originally a social worker, Susie has worked at WPHS for six years. She felt the call to animal welfare after watching a program on Animal Planet that featured trainers helping homeless dogs become rehabilitated and adopted.

"I thought I had a connection with animals. I had never met a dog that didn't like me," she said. "I was tired of the sadness of social work. It burns you out."

As the front line for surrendered pets and an impromptu triage nurse, Susie has found animal welfare exhausting in its own right. Black and white photos of canine faces were lined up above her computer, a "Wall of Shame" erected to those she couldn't save.

Days before a long-awaited summer vacation, Susie was summoned to the WPHS parking lot. A man had driven in and told the staff that he had sick puppies. The pit bull/ rottweiler mixes were just four months old. To avoid cross contamination, the puppies were tested for parvo in the parking lot. One by one they tested positive. One by one, Susie brought a puppy to the staff veterinarian, who euthanized them on the spot in her arms.

"I can't forget, when I was walking out there, picking them up and looking into their eyes. It'll never leave me as long as I live," she said. "Animals don't know that we're doing all that we can. I don't think they know how sorry we are."

Whenever Susie tried explaining to an owner surrendering the family pet that doing so often leads to euthanasia due to lack of space or myriad reasons, the response can be downright violent. One person told her she was damned and going to hell. Another got so out of control that a supervisor had to be called in.

"Nobody ever thinks the right thing is to euthanize their animal, they think because we're a humane society we're supposed to save all the animals that come in. People take no burden on themselves, so I'm an easy target," Susie said. "If I didn't have my nephews, who are my life, and time with my sister and friends who volunteer here, I'd lose it."

Susie's not giving up though. Her next plan of attack was to form a coalition of volunteers and put together a community action plan with an outreach program that not only educates about adoption, but provides low- or no-cost spaying and neutering and vaccinations.

"If people can't feed their kids, they're surely not going to get their animals vaccinated and spayed or neutered," she said. "We have to provide them with every resource we can."

***

Emotionally stunned from my meetings and the tour, I was grateful to get back to the office area to pick up Loren. Though she had made herself at home on the carpeted floor and friends with everyone that crossed her path during the two hours I was gone, she still perked right up when she saw me. I thanked Gretchen and quickly led Loren back through the lobby and out the doors in a daze.

"Oh, how sweet, was she adopted?" I heard someone ask as the doors shut behind us.

Once in the truck, I hugged Loren tight and kissed her snout before breaking down in tears. Inside that building were 400 or 500 animals, half of whom probably wouldn't make it out alive.

On one hand, I loved the efforts of the staff, the outreach, the actions taken in the face of an almost impossible situation. On the other hand, it made any Pollyanna-ish fantasies I held onto about the day of no more homeless pets coming in my lifetime screech to an abrupt halt.

I had been to a few Los Angeles shelters to search for my cat Pookie, who went missing in the '94 Northridge earthquake (and found his way home two weeks later), but I never made it past the kennels. That was depressing enough to contemplate, let alone whatever went on in the back rooms. Not to mention the horror stories I heard from Brittany Foundation volunteers who regularly pulled dogs from L.A. County shelters, especially Lancaster, where Loren was from.

I knew the statistics. Every year, between four and six million American pets are killed, euthanized, or put to sleep, whatever grammatical term we humans like to use define the unnecessary murder of healthy companion animals. Before I had been to New York City and Pittsburgh, the numbers were intellectual and distant. Now I had seen the cold truth firsthand, and the statistics had faces. Sweet, anxious, silly, hopeful faces. It was almost too much to bear.

Loren looked at me with soulful eyes and I envied her, that she couldn't comprehend the challenges facing dogs like her and the emotional toll it took on the humans who cared.

For a minute, I wished I didn't know, that I could shut the lid on this Pandora's box and go back to blissful semi-ignorance.

Four to six million. Dead. Every year. 400,000 a month, 14,000 a day. 584 every hour. Killed.

Why did we bother, really? It was all just a drop in the bucket.

Breathing deeply, I blinked back my tears and saw the answer in the seat next to me. You do what you can, one dog at a time.

Even if she'd never found a family to adopt her, Loren had The Brittany Foundation to go home to and all of us volunteers who loved her. Me most of all. Whereas I used to feel sorry for her, living at a rescue, I realized Loren was actually one of the lucky ones.

***

Penguin madness had spilled out into the streets of Pittsburgh as we made our way south to meet Daisy Faelten Balawejder and Amy Dengler, founder and board member of Hello Bully, a non-profit advocacy organization, for lunch.

The hockey team's Stanley Cup victory parade had brought something close to 400,000 rabid Penguins fans to the city center. Young and old, tall and short, fat and skinny, it was a sea of black and white Penguins shirts, caps, banners, and signs spilling like a slow mud slide along the streets and sidewalks.

Cars were stuck for what seemed like forever, lights turning from red to green with little to no movement. I started to panic. I had no idea where I was, let alone any shortcuts that might lessen the hellish wait and get us to our destination somewhere close to on time.

About 10 minutes before we were supposed to meet, I called Daisy's cell phone and explained the situation. She passed me to Amy, who shared some detour ideas, and said they were happy to wait for us, however long it took.

We arrived an hour late to the Doublewide Grill, a funky south Pittsburgh diner in a neighborhood that reminded me of an East Coast version of Venice, California. Lanky, young tattooed types and college students were milling about vintage store and tattoo shops, while the restaurants and bars were abuzz with activity.

Daisy, a buxom fair-skinned redhead, and Amy, a petite brunette, waved us over to the patio, making a fuss over Loren and giving her kisses before requesting a bowl of water from the waiter. You can always tell true bully lovers. They're shameless about making out with strange dogs, just as brazen as the dogs themselves.

We settled in and ordered. Balawejder is a vegan and Dengler ordered shrimp, but I went carnivore and ordered a BBQ pork sandwich, then felt guilty and questioned my decision and their impression of me. While I try not to eat pork and beef more than occasionally, I can't seem to resist when I'm on the road. It's the last vice I cling to, since I don't drink or smoke anymore, eating whatever I want instead of maybe what's healthy or humane.

"Don't worry about it," Daisy assured me. "I used to eat meat, too."

Our talk quickly turned to Hello Bully and their efforts. Daisy founded the organization in 2005 with her husband John, after the death of their first pit bull, Kaneda, from cancer.

Since then, Hello Bully has placed 25 pit bulls, mostly strays or owner surrenders, into loving homes. They put their dogs through a series of tests and evaluations to determine temperament and only the highly people-friendly make the cut.

"We want Hello Bully alumni to be great representatives of the breed," Daisy said.

Hello Bully has seven board members and 25 volunteers that staff outreach programs such as Pit Fix Plus, which includes free vaccination and spay/neuter (or "speuter" as Daisy likes to call it) vouchers, as well as training and exercise resources that provide pit owners with the tools to deal with unwanted behaviors.

"If we can give people management techniques, we can avoid getting these dogs turned in to shelters," Amy said. "About half of the pit owners we deal with decide to keep their dogs."

The rest are often fostered by the Hello Bully network. Dengler has two pit bulls; the male is a therapy dog. Balawejder's pit pack includes Miko and Mizuki.

Funds for the programs and foster resources are raised by several small events and a new gala, called "Lovers Not Fighters," which was recently held at a local restaurant and attracted close to 300 guests; it raised more than $10,000.

"We had lawyers, doctors, mechanics, and tattoo artists. It was a true melting pot," Daisy said. "It was just a devoted group of pit bull owners and lovers bonding over their affection for the breed."

Daisy, a graphic artist by trade, designed the Hello Bully logo as a friendly, iconic cartoon of the breed that will soon be featured in comic books and other educational materials.

"We're hoping to get into schools with Hello Bully," she said. "It can make a big difference when kids come home and tell their parents, 'I got to meet Hello Bully today!'"

Their five-year plan includes opening a non-traditional shelter where adoptable dogs live in a home rather than kennel environment. They see it as a "halfway house," so that the transition to being homed won't be such a shock for the dog or its new owner.

"Temperament tests and evaluations are done while the dog's in a high-stress shelter, where they often fail," Daisy explained. "We want to give them a better chance to succeed."

Unfortunately, as Amy illustrated, it's an uphill battle. "Some people still have the impression that shelter dogs are defective, that they have to go to a breeder for a dog, even if it's an ad in the Pennysaver from some guy that's doing it in his backyard," she said.

"You can't stop stupid," Balawejder said.

Nor can you save all the pits in Pittsburgh. Murphy, a large black and white two-year-old male, was picked up by a dogcatcher from a neighboring county and taken to a Pittsburgh shelter.

When Daisy went to visit him the following Saturday, Murphy gave her the typical bully intro: lots of wiggling, followed by kisses through the bars of his kennel. Since he was not yet neutered or vaccinated, Daisy had to wait until the next day to walk Murphy.

After a Penguins game, Balawejder and her husband headed to the shelter on Sunday with a peanut-butter and biscuit-stuffed Kong for Murphy. When they arrived, Daisy immediately sensed something was wrong. "I looked for someone to take me back to see Murphy. When I saw the attendant's face, I knew," she recalled.

Murphy had failed the dog aggression portion of the behavioral evaluation. Miserably. With both males and females. The shelter could not adopt him out to the public, only to a rescue under a "dangerous dog" waiver. Since the Balawejders had two dogs, including a female that was dog aggressive, they couldn't adopt Murphy themselves.

"In a perfect world, we could place Murphy with someone who would work on training and management. We would give him a life, where he was never set up to fail," Daisy said. "But most shelters are understaffed with too few volunteers. They do not have the resources to deal with the more dog aggressive pit bulls. Placing dogs that show that level of aggression is a liability not only to the shelter, but for every responsible pit owner who worries that one day BSL might come knocking on their door."

Daisy went to Murphy's kennel and sat with him for the last time, giving him the Kong. Murphy licked at it for a moment, then came right back to Daisy for kisses.

As her eyes burned from a flood of tears and melted mascara, Daisy held Murphy. This is what she told him:

"I am so, so sorry Murphy. I am so sorry that everyone in your life has failed you. They used you, bred you and discarded you. No one ever cared for the stress sores on your feet.

"It is likely that you never knew the joy of rolling in the spring grass after getting a bath, that you never had someone bury their face in the folds of your neck and smell the delicious scent of a freshly bathed dog. You were never on a Christmas card, or photographed and shown off from a wallet or pretty frame. No one ever loved you, Murphy, and you just kept on loving us, hoping that someone, someday would see you.

Daisy and Murphy say goodbye

"I saw you, Murphy. I saw your love and your gentle soul and the soft, luscious adoration in your eyes. For a very short time, I hope you knew that you were loved. You will always be loved by me, Murphy. I will cherish your photos and memories and the knowledge that you are going somewhere special, where you will romp in green grass and roll in flowered fields…and someday, Murphy, I will see you again."

Murphy's ashes rest upon Daisy's desk. His name and likeness, adorned with angel wings, are tattooed on her feet, where Daisy's own dogs curl up nightly, a permanent reminder to keep fighting.

The Humane and the Insane

Following a brief overnight in Charleston, West Virginia, we had a 400 mile trek to Indianapolis, where we were scheduled to meet with Christine Jeschke, a friend of Stacey's at Animal Farm, who helped run the Indianapolis Humane Society.

Since we headed this way in large part due to the breed ban in Ohio, I was horrified when Gidget sent us toward a Cincinnati highway. So much so, I pulled over and actually consulted my atlas, which, even as geographically challenged as I am, is a rarity. I even stopped at a gas station and asked a truck driver for his opinion, just to make sure I was on the right path.

Our new route took us through Louisville, Kentucky, which looked like a really cool city, rife with independent music shops, book stores, ethnic restaurants, and boutiques, surrounded by the lush Kentucky landscape and charming Southern architecture. We stopped at Homemade Ice Cream and Pie Kitchen, for a hummus and spring mix sandwich, as well as a piece of mixed berry pie, which I wolfed down on the interstate. Great food.

Indiana wasn't as flat or as dry as I expected. The rolling hills were less hilly, but the trees were still there. Loren and I cruised into town around 5 p.m. and stopped at West Park for a stroll. The area we stayed at, near the Pyramids, was very suburban and the park gorgeously green.

A wooded path looped around a little lake, festooned with lily pads, ducks skimming along the surface. Loren, though hot, was fascinated by the new environment, sniffing along contentedly before the humidity took over. She took many a break, under whatever shade she could find. Taking her cue, I laid out too, for a few minutes, my hand resting on Loren's back, and gazed upward. There's something special about the Midwest sky, so open, so blue, and that day, big fluffy clouds abounded.

"Beautiful, isn't it, Boogie?" I asked her. Loren's wide grin and half-closed eyes were answer enough. She agreed.

For dinner, I had to try a regional specialty made popular in Ohio, spaghetti and chili. I ordered it four-way, which means meat sauce, cheese, and onions over pasta. The sauce had a cinnamon tang, similar to what you find in moussaka, which I found really tasty. I also ate a Greek salad, to balance out the damage. Ha.

The skies turned dark the next morning, when we went to Indy Humane, as it is known. I was immediately struck by the spacious gated play yard in the front, complete with a picnic bench and dog houses. Inside the facility, it was warm and inviting, cheerful even, painted in bright colors. It looked more like an upscale vet's office than a shelter.

We were greeted warmly by staff and Loren immediately made herself at home in an employee's office while Christine gave me a tour.

She had just started at Indy Humane in December, 2008, but her passion and commitment were palpable, as Christine had been involved in the animal welfare movement for over a decade.

We looked at the cats first. "The policy here used to be to euthanize cats with feline HIV, but we've instituted a new program and have adopted out eight since then," she said.

Christine Jeschke and adoptable cats at Indy Humane

Like all the shelters I visited, cat intakes were more prevalent than that of dogs, especially in the summertime, the peak of kitten season. Though admittedly a dog person, I had loved my Pookie and I was fond of Wayde's cat, even though he called her Pretty Princess and Gorgeous. Wayde's pet name for me is Sathe.

There was a kittenish version of Pookie there, an orange tabby whom Christine interacted with. Many cats were waiting in the back, until a spot on the adoption floor opened up. In the dog areas, I was happy and surprised to see many of the kennels empty.

"We had a huge level of adoptions this weekend and last," Christine said. "We're putting in calls to other shelters to bring their dogs here."

One reason the adoptions were so high was a well-publicized puppy mill bust, which brought 20 survivors to Indy Humane. "Those dogs were snapped up in no time," Christine said. "Best of all, all our little dogs went with them, because of the publicity."

Of the big dogs, a nine-year old purebred German Shepherd was one of the sadder stories. His owners, who claimed they paid $15,000 for the dog and brought all his papers to Indy Humane, had surrendered him once they lost their home. On the opposite end of the spectrum, a trio of chocolate and black lab-pit mix puppies played in an adorable tangle inside their small crate.

Thankfully, Indy Humane's overall adoption rate is extremely high, over 90 percent. Of the dogs they take in, approximately 10 percent or less are pit bulls due to their suburban location and demographic.

"Go to the city and the kennels are overflowing with pits," Christine said. "We bring a lot of them to Indy Humane, but have to be careful not to overdo it. Some of our long-term adopters don't want to see high numbers of bully breeds. We have to keep it balanced."

For the harder to place animals, Christine, a married mother of a three-year old adopted son, as well as four dogs, four cats, and fish, goes the extra mile. The woman amazed me, not only because of her commitment, but because she had perfect hair and makeup. Where did Christine find the time? Apparently, by not sleeping much.

"I'm up until midnight, looking at our inventory, trying to find foster homes, rescue groups, whoever I can find, to take our dogs and cats," she said.

Several members of Indy Humane's staff belong to a non-profit pit bull advocacy group called Indy Pit Crew, which provides training, free spay/neuter vouchers, and other resources to owners.

"Give me some love, Nina...mwah!"

"We'll offer people free dog food to get their dog spayed or neutered," said Nina Gaither, Indy Humane behaviorist and Indy Pit Crew volunteer. "Whatever it takes."

Nina and Lisa Stewart, also an Indy Humane behaviorist and Indy Pit Crew volunteer, are proud parents of pit bulls themselves. Stella rides around with Lisa in her "Indy Pit Crew" emblazoned SUV, cheeks flapping in the wind.

Coal, a gorgeous gray and white bully taken during a drug bust, has a slight, silly underbite and awesome demeanor. So much so that his mama Nina, who also had a male pit bull named Lex, uses him for temperament evaluations at the shelter. "Coal gets along with everyone, he's just a solid, solid dog," Nina said.

Indy Pit Crew is just one way Indy Humane is partnering with the community to benefit its pets. Plans are in the works for a resource center, closer to lower-income zip codes, that will provide owners with options such as free food, veterinary care, and training as an alternative to turning their pets in to a shelter.

Until then, Indy Humane is focused on using online social networking, such as Facebook and email blast programs, to increase its visibility in the area and encourage its residents to adopt, rather than shop for pets. Their "Adopt 500 Animals in May" campaign met its goal, albeit slightly late, on June 4.

Tristan Schmid, Indy Humane's communications manager, realized the power of online marketing before he went to work at the shelter. At his previous company, located in a lower income area, co-workers would often find stray kittens and dogs, especially pit bulls, in the parking lot and just beyond.

"I started posting them on Craigslist and also sending out emails to staff whenever a dog or cat would be found," Tristan said. "At least a dozen animals were adopted out that way."

Loren was present at our meeting, her paws resting on Tristan's lap, her head near his for prime kissing opportunities. He petted her as we discussed the complex nuances of the animal welfare issue: education, low cost or free spay and neuter, providing owners with the resources they need to keep their pet, and what an uphill battle it felt like at times.

"It's easy to preach to the choir," I said to Tristan. "It's reaching those outside the circle that's so hard."

"Yeah, I know. A lot of people in this country don't understand why there's a movement to help homeless pets when humans are suffering, too," Tristan said. "But I believe that we have to have compassion and recognize these creatures as the living, sentient beings that they are. Otherwise, what hope is there for us as a society?"

My feelings mirror Tristan's. When we turn domesticated animals away or dump them or mistreat them, we not only violate their trust and right to a decent life, we create a far-reaching social problem with a shameful, unacceptable solution. The killing of millions of homeless pets each year.

I wished there was no need for me to volunteer at the Brittany Foundation or take a dog across country to promote adoption. I wished the problem didn't exist at all. Unfortunately, like abuse, addiction, famine, war and all the other horrible things in this world, the situation is manmade.

At Nina's suggestion, Loren and I drove to the downtown area and went for a stroll on the canals that start on 10th Street. What an oasis in a big city, the water calm and serene, surrounded by sidewalks and lawns on either side.

Apartments and town homes faced the canals. Couples walked by hand in hand, one lounging on a bench, the girl with her head in her boyfriend's lap.

An older man walked his small fluffy white dog while joggers jammed by, iPods in place.

The scene was really peaceful, until a group of young teenage boys rode by us on their bikes. One of them made a kissing sound when he spotted Loren, who nervously leaned against my legs as they approached.

"I'd do your dog in the butt!" he screamed as his friends laughed.

OK, that was a first…and hopefully a last. I predicted a lot of therapy in this kid's future.

Craving something semi-healthy and meatless, I spotted a falafel place a half mile from our hotel and placed an order. As I waited, a man came up to me, commenting on my Indy Pit Crew T-shirt, given to me by Lisa and Nina.

"My wife's dog keeps having babies. I don't know why," he said with a smile.

"Well," I said, unsuccessfully trying to hold back my sarcasm. "You could have your dogs spayed and neutered."

"Oh, I know. But my wife's from the country and she'd never go for that," he responded. "People in Rockville, where I live, want Yorkie puppies."

"There are lots of great little dogs for adoption at the shelter, right here, at Indy Humane," I responded.

"Yeah, but people don't want to drive all the way out here and there aren't any shelters where we live," he said.

He continued to tell me about his dogs, his barn cats, the country way of life in general. I just stood there, growing slightly numb as one does during an unreciprocated conversation. Finally, the cook came out and handed the man his bag of food.

His parting comment shocked me.

"I appreciate what you're doing," the man said. "Things might change someday. It's just going to take a long time."

Hungry and tired, I took Loren for a potty break before going to the room. She was not ready to go back in yet, not only stopping in her tracks, but crossing her legs, too. I was in no mood. After trying nicely to cajole her in the door, my food growing colder and my hunger increasing by the minute, I dragged her in.

Loren gave me a dirty look, a pout even, and for the first time on our entire trip, did not jump up on the bed with me when I called her. I tried and tried, but it was no use. She laid out on the floor near the foot of the bed instead. She was clearly over me. I couldn't help it, I was hurt. I cried. I was all alone. Thousands of miles from home. Without the comfort of my best canine girlfriend to get me through.

I finally fell asleep, when the phone rang. It was my boyfriend, three hours behind in California.

"Loren doesn't love me anymore," I said and explained the situation.

"Aw, you poor thing," Wayde said. "You're really alone, huh?"

"Yes," I said sadly.

"Don't worry, she'll probably jump up on the bed in the middle of the night," he said.

After we hung up, I went to the bathroom. When I got back into bed, there was a red and white lump lying near my pillow. I kissed Loren's head and cried a little more.

"Thank you," I said and held her close.

Go West!

We left Indianapolis with no particular destination in mind, just to drive as far as we could into Wisconsin. I was in particularly good spirits, determined not to let my occasional homesickness get in the way of the present. Time would pass nonetheless. I had better enjoy every minute.

This spirit held up until we hit Chicago and got stuck in two hours of traffic. In the rain. Having to pee like never before. It was miserable. Despite having fantasized about a few ways I might be able to relieve myself in the car without getting caught, I couldn't go through with it and pulled over to a grocery store. Sometimes peeing, when you've held it for far too long, is better than sex.

By the time we made it to Tomah, Wisconsin, my caffeine buzz was gone and huge clouds were rolling in. As we checked into our hotel, it started pouring fiercely. The clerk said a town 20 minutes away had quarter-sized hail and that we should brace ourselves. While that never came to pass, the skies never really brightened until the next day. Loren and I took a rain day, watching TV and snuggling until we both fell asleep.

We headed out bright and early for North Dakota. I was coveting a cheese store across the road and couldn't believe my good fortune when they opened at 8:30 a.m. Wisconsin is not only a very pretty state, it has entire stores devoted to cheese! That's awesome.

I perused the aisles and settled on some cheese curds, a garlic beef stick, and some caramel pecan clusters called "Snappers." Loren gratefully accepted my offers of the first two, licking the goodies gently off my palm. The snacks sustained us both until we made it to St. Paul, the skyline poking out in the distance, becoming clearer as we came to our off-ramp to the Tavern on Grand.

St. Paul is a neat, clean city, with mature trees shading the sidewalks and tall, narrow houses of brick and iron lining the road. There was a college town feel here, like Asheville, which, I've come to realize, is my favorite type of city. I found a shady spot for Loren and headed to the tavern across the street.

Of course, I had to order the pike, as their logo says "Minnesota's State Restaurant Serving Minnesota's State Fish." As I ordered it, I asked the waiter a question, the reporter in me rarely resting, not even on vacation.

"If this is Minnesota's state fish, why do you import yours from Canada?" I pointed to the menu where it listed this information.

He smiled. "The fish from Canada is consistent in size and quality. We can't say that about the fish from our lakes, unfortunately," he said. "We serve the most pike of anywhere in the country. Something like two-thirds of the pike caught is sold right here."

"Wow," I responded.

The waiter recommended the pike grilled (it also comes fried or blackened) and I wasn't disappointed. The flaky, delicate fish was moist and clean-tasting, lightly spiced, and enhanced with a good dollop of rich, buttery Béarnaise sauce, which to me, is the savory equivalent of chocolate, as in, you can't go wrong with it. Accompanied by simple grilled potatoes and steamed fresh vegetables, it was one of the best meals of the trip.

Feeling better about the world, we barreled on to Fargo, North Dakota, and stopped at a hotel. They said they were booked and I was glad to have a reason to leave. It felt weird, all that open space, that nothingness, filled in with big box stores and restaurant chains. People were lingering about the hotel, smoking. The whole scene said tweaker to me.

About 50 miles later, though I was still amped on too many Arnold Palmers, I came to my senses and found us a place to stay. I know that weird state of believing you can drive forever - I once made it from Portland, Oregon to home in one day, driving close to a thousand miles, and started hallucinating the last three hours. Better safe than sorry.

The only room available had a Jacuzzi, so I ponied up an extra few bucks and took it. It felt like kind of a waste on just me, but I enjoyed relaxing in the nice hot bubbles before calling it a night. Loren seemed to love me again. It took a little coaxing to get her on the bed, but she jumped up, stretching out, letting me rub her belly until I heard her snore and drifted off myself. We both slept like babies.

Driving from Jamestown to Billings was a challenge, especially without a Starbucks in sight, but we did it. Wide open spaces. For hours and hours. Huge sky. Massive clouds. It was pretty, in its own way, but not very stimulating. Thank God for the books on tape that I had picked up near Tomah. I don't know how else I would have made it through.

Salem Sue and the Toyota

Of course, there were also the exciting side trips, like seeing Salem Sue, the world's largest fake Holstein cow, looming over the small town of New Salem. The entrance gate was deserted, so we drove up the gravelly hill to see her up close. She was a big girl, indeed. Loren had no interest in getting out of the truck and meeting Sue. She looked up at the huge creature with wide eyes and furrowed brows from the cab, so I got out and took a photo without her, just the Toyota and Salem Sue.

The landscape changed near the Montana border as we passed the off ramp for the Theodore Roosevelt State park. It was beginning to look more like New Mexico and Arizona, the flat, leveled-off mountains in a kaleidescope of colors; red, green, beige, even purple. It made my eyes happy. Little patches of water began to appear, too. Now it felt like we were heading West and home. The time zone changed, too, as did the atmosphere. No more humidity. My hair was manageable again. Yeah!

We stayed in Billings the first night, leaving the next morning for Missoula, but had to stop for an oil change first. It seemed we found the most dog-friendly service station around at Cor Automotive, where Loren was warmly greeted with pets, smiles, and enthusiasm.

"We love dogs here," Tom, the manager, said. "I have five myself, all rescues."

"I get all my dogs from the Prison PAWS program," John, the owner, said.

"What's that?" I asked.

"They pair shelter dogs with women prisoners, who train them before they go into homes," he replied.

"I love it," I said. "What a great idea."

"Yeah, it gives the prisoners something to do, something to care for and be compassionate about," John said. "And the dogs that come out of there are fantastic, really well-trained."

I took Loren around the block for a 20 minute-walk while my car was worked on. The area was rife with rundown rentals and industrial buildings. We headed back to the shop, where Loren was presented with a bowl of water and some dog biscuits. She settled contentedly on the cool concrete floor and greeted everyone that came in.

"I think she wants to be your shop dog," I told the guys. They laughed. The three men gathered around Loren for a photo and she sat proudly at their feet, as at home in the oil-stained garage as she was at the Novotel in NYC. As long as there are people around, Loren's a happy dog.

Tom's wife Darlynn, a mail carrier, came in and saw my truck. "Think you have enough paw prints on there?" she asked, laughing.

When I explained what we were doing, she smiled brightly.

"I fought against the breed specific legislation they were trying to pass here a few years back," she said. "I told them, as a mail carrier, that I had way more problems with poodles than pit bulls."

"Did it pass?" I asked.

"Nope," she said proudly.

"Right on," I said.

On the way to Missoula, we stopped in Bozeman, another little college town with great restaurants and stores lining the streets. I spotted a patio adjacent to a funky, lively diner and pulled over to ask if they allowed dogs. They did, so Loren and I had lunch at the Garage Soup Shack.

Considering the name, I had to order the soup, a rich, not-too-thick bowl of delicious clam chowder that had an unexpected zing, along with a refreshing spring mix salad and a tasty grilled cheese sandwich with tomato and bacon.

I snapped off the bacon ends and gave them to Loren, who took them gently and thwacked her tail. Maybe bacon was almost as good as affection to her…or even better.

Snow-capped mountains begin to peek through the clouds and my heart lifted. I love that sight. It was cold, too, in the 50s and 60s, depending on whether or not you were in the sun, but I didn't mind. Better than the heat and humidity of the Great Plains. Loren the hot dog seemed to like it too. The West Coast canine was longer panting and scratching as much as she had been in the south.

After the 350 mile journey, we were both happy to see our hotel in Missoula. There was an American Kennel Club dog show the next day, so we couldn't have a first floor room; it was overrun with dogs and their owners. We went up to the third floor, Loren totally adept at navigating both the stairs and the elevator.

As we went on our last walk of the night through the low scrubby hills adjacent to the parking lot, a minivan with a traveling kennel towed behind it pulled up in the parking lot. The crude wooden contraption had six tiny compartments, each containing a Brittany spaniel. The dogs poked their heads through the roughly cut holes that acted as windows. Hmm, I thought. Loren the shelter dog, with her pillow and comforter stuffed cab, was traveling in higher style than the show dogs.

There was an email from Bernice of Animal Farm Foundation when we got back to our room. Turned out Loren, my pit bull ambassador, was actually part American Staffordshire Terrier and part Bulldog. I called her a bully from that moment on.

***

Driving close to 1,500 miles in three days wore me out. That and I had developed a rash, which, after ruling out bedbugs, I determined to be an allergy of some kind. I self-prescribed Benadryl to get rid of it, which made me even more exhausted, so the 170 or so miles to Coeur D'Alene felt twice that, but we made it.

I had planned on staying at a budget motel off the freeway, but once I got a view of Coeur D'Alene Lake, I thought, no way. If you're here, you should do it right. So we drove along the east side, praying to find a cute little lake view hotel for under $100 a night. I just wanted to sit and look at the water for a while.

Bennett Bay Inn appeared just a few miles up the road. I pulled over and not only was it pet-friendly, there was a room for us! It was $85 with a Jacuzzi tub. Each room was decorated in a different theme, kind of like a mini-Madonna Inn, the famous hotel in San Luis Obispo. Ours was "The Roman Room" with faux plaster walls, tiny Grecian statues, and plastic vines in every corner. The Jacuzzi had pillars. It had a fantastic view of the lake. It was perfect.

"Romantic, huh, Loren?" I laughed and held her close as we briefly relaxed on the queen-sized bed. She sighed.

Before passing out for a long nap, we went to O'Shay's, a quaint little pub and restaurant with a patio located just before the entrance to town. Our waitress, Sarah, was afraid of pit bulls as she had been bitten by one when she was 20. It was her brother's roommate's dog and it was old, blind, and not familiar with her. When she came in the front yard, he jumped up and bit her in the hand, requiring several stitches.

"I don't blame you for being scared," I told her. "But Loren would never hurt a person, unless they were trying to hurt me. Oh, and she's a Staffordshire/Bulldog mix, if that makes you feel any better."

Unmoved, Sarah still kept her distance, though she was kind enough to bring Loren some water and grilled chicken, handing both to me to give to Loren.

My sister Heidi was bitten by a dog when I was three or four, on her lip, requiring stitches. Somehow, I always thought it was a German Shepherd. I was so fearful of the breed throughout my life that it was obvious to any shepherds in my midst; during a pet-sitting job as a teen, the German Shepherd on the premises, ironically named Pal, jumped up and bit a plate-sized hole in my sweater.

When I told Heidi about the Pal incident and explained I was afraid of German shepherds because of what happened to her, she responded, with typical older sister exasperation, "Michelle, that was a poodle!" So, who was I to fault someone who actually had been bitten by a particular breed?

In the evening, Loren and I relaxed on the patio and watched the sun turn the lake a shimmering silver before disappearing into the ebony sky. The Bennett Bay Inn had several Adirondack style chairs and benches for us to lounge on and we had the place to ourselves, so I slipped my arm around her and held her close.

"How rad is this, girl?" I asked her. Loren returned my gaze, licked my cheek, then turned to look at the lake, too, both of us content to sit in silence. Though I originally thought Asheville would be my top town in the U.S. to live after this trip, I think it has been replaced by Coeur D'Alene. What a gorgeous place.

The next morning, we got up bright and early, and took a long walk along the paved bike path that encircled miles of the lake, which is the site for the annual Ironman Triathlon. The docks groaned in the water like beseeched animals at times, making Loren cock her head. She sniffed and even jogged a little bit, looking up in fascination as a woman with a big fro of permed blonde hair skated by us or when bicyclists would whiz by from behind.

"Is it time for ice cream yet?"

We headed out for the 37-mile or so famous scenic drive. I had stopped by Java on Sherman, a hopping coffeehouse and bakery in the middle of downtown, first for provisions, a bagel with lox and cream cheese, a massive blueberry scone, and an Arnold Palmer. The drive was amazing, offering a view of the incredible bridge that perched above the lake, as well as some dazzling waterfront properties and the many boats docked alongside them. Mountains and water; there is no better combo for beauty and harmony, in my opinion.

The two-hour round trip had me worn out, so we took a three-hour nap this time, Loren snuggled up against me. We awoke around 4 p.m. and went for another walk before going back to O'Shay's for a dinner of Shepherd's Pie and salad. The pie was delicious, a huge slab of rustic mashed potatoes, vegetables, and savory ground beef smothered with a rich brown gravy. It comforted my soul. Loren ate her grilled chicken breast with relish, so she seemed pretty satisfied, too.

For dessert, I had spotted a homemade ice cream stand called Michael's, so I pulled up for a vanilla scoop for Loren and a cookies and cream with hot fudge for me, which we polished off in the car before heading back to our place.

The night ended with us in the Adirondack bench, Loren laying by my feet as I read, before we retired to watch *Wipeout* and crash.

Loren really was the perfect travel companion. Never a complaint. Okay, so she was occasionally stubborn about where she wanted to walk and it could be annoying waiting for her to go to the bathroom (already), but other than that, Loren had been the best. I already started to miss her.

***

We bid Coeur d'Alene adieu the next morning, watching as the sun poked its way out from the water and into the sky. I would've been sad to leave, except that we were heading to Mukilteo, Washington, to meet with Michelle Vincent and her husband Randy for the night. Michelle and I had worked together for many years in California, developing a strong friendship before she and Randy departed for Washington in 2008. The following morning, we were all headed to Deception Pass for camping with my parents, who were driving an RV from their home in Idaho Falls.

Mukilteo is on the coast of Washington, set against the Puget Sound, and my friend's house was a quarter mile from the shore. Michelle and Randy had a 26-foot RV parked in their circular driveway that would act as our home for the evening.

Their two dogs, Cherokee, an Irish Setter, and Cheyenne, an English Setter, were very excited to meet Loren. We made the intro, with Cheyenne, the younger, less high-strung of the two.

Cheyenne, who sports liver colored patches and a fluffy white tuft of hair on her forehead, darted out and started sniffing Loren immediately. Loren's tail wagged at first, but within two seconds, her scruff began to stand up and I could see and hear the growl coming. I pulled her away from Cheyenne and we retreated to the camper for a good night's sleep, which was easy to do in the peaceful suburban neighborhood.

We awoke the next morning and after stopping off at a killer half-priced book store, where I made at least a half dozen selections, drove to the Whidbey Island Ferry. I didn't realize that we were supposed to be in the far right lane and accidentally tried to cut in line.

"YOO HOO! You need to turn around and get in back of the line," the toll taker yelled at me.

Never having done this before, I was a bit embarrassed and a little angry. It was unintentional. However, I've been taught to take accountability for my actions.

"Sorry about that," I said sheepishly when I pulled up to the same booth after 10 minutes of waiting. "I've never taken the ferry before and didn't know how it was done."

"Well, there are signs everywhere!" the woman said, with a phony smile on her face.

My own smile dropped. I hate it when you not only apologize to deaf ears, but are tried to be made to look even more stupid than you already felt. She got the death stare from me and no response.

The toll taker looked at the magnets on my truck and Loren in the passenger seat.

"I see you do a lot for the animals," she said, handing me my change.

"Yeah," I responded flatly, after a pause, turning my head away. Loren and my dogs have taught me this trick. Like, you have hurt my feelings and I won't acknowledge you anymore. For them, it lasts about 10 seconds. For me, it can last up to 10 years.

There was a half-hour wait, where we watched a drug-sniffing German Shepherd do his job and people get out of their cars for ice cream. We stayed put, not wanting to do anything else wrong.

It was strange to drive onto the ferry, which is basically a big, floating parking lot. When we pulled away from the dock, it was a sensation of not knowing whether you were the one moving or watching something being moved away from you. The ride lasted about 15 minutes, then we were on Whidbey Island.

My boss, who has a part-time vacation home here, had recommended we stop at Seabolt's for crab cakes, as they tout having the best around. It was about 38 miles from our ferry landing, which took us through woodsy landscape, small restaurants and businesses, and some gorgeous shoreline. Seabolt's was only 10 miles from Deception Pass, our ultimate destination. Inside, it was part restaurant/part seafood counter, with local fish on display and contented customers chowing down on fish and chips.

I ordered the clam chowder and crab cake. The former was really delicious; rich, thick, stocked with a good amount of tender clams and potatoes. The latter was OK; a fat, puffy fried disc with shredded crabmeat and solid flavor. After the SoBo/Baltimore experience, however, any crab cake would be a letdown. It was, hands down, the best thing I ate on the whole trip.

Tall redwoods began to appear as we neared Deception Pass, which featured a majestic lake on the way to the campgrounds. My parents, Jim and Rosie, were already there with their two dogs, Annie and Sammy. I had warned them in advance that Loren wasn't too fond of other dogs.

This was my first time meeting Annie, whom my parents had rescued from an Idaho Falls shelter in February. She's a cute little terrier, or terror, mix with fluffy, multi-colored fur; feisty, funny, and altogether adorable. Sammy, meanwhile, is an 85-pound golden shepherd/possible Rhodesian Ridgeback mix my parents adopted from a litter of farm puppies in Colorado. Something of a gentle giant, Sammy can lapse into herding instinct on occasion and want to chase down joggers and small kids on bicycles. My mom has to be on guard when walking him, which is a challenge since she doesn't weigh much more than he does.

"Who's the new girl?

Sammy and Annie, experienced campers, were staked close to my parents' trailer, so I placed Loren on her post at least 20 feet from them. Sammy was giving her the eye for a while, partial curiosity, partial warning, partial lust perhaps?

I couldn't blame him. Loren was a beautiful dog. I reached down and patted Loren on the head. She basked in the partial sunlight that filtered onto her blanket and rolled onto her side for a nap.

"Isn't Loren just the prettiest dog you've ever seen?" I asked my father.

He paused. "Well, she's alright, but she's not really my kind of dog," my dad replied.

"What?" I said incredulously, a mocking tone in my voice. "No way, she's the coolest."

"To each their own," my dad said.

True. But I think bullies are the cutest dogs ever. I adore their markings, their spotted pink or blue noses, their silly demeanors, their strong bodies, their kissy-poo muzzles, their soft hearts. For the life of me, I can't understand why everyone doesn't feel this way, but love, whether it be human or canine, is almost impossible to explain.

Michelle and Randy arrived later in the afternoon. Since they both are fisherman, my dad and Randy headed out for a quick trip to the lake while Michelle finished setting up camp. Randy must have been a good luck charm, because my dad, who is notorious for rarely catching anything, brought back a trout, which he fried up as a snack for all of us.

"You should take Randy fishing with you all the time, Jim," my mother said.

"Ha ha, Rosie," he replied.

For dinner, Mom had prepared spaghetti with homemade meat sauce, garlic bread and salad, while Michelle had made chicken marsala. Camping is awesome when you have someone a) feeding you great meals, b) letting you sleep in their well-equipped trailer and c) giving you tools and ingredients to roast marshmallows over a fire at night. Loren and I crashed on the pullout couch in Randy and Michelle's RV, getting our usual eight hours, snuggling extra tight. The Washington air was chilly and damp.

"So, Rosie, this dog walks into a bar..."

The next morning, Michelle's friend Kim arrived and we all went to the North Beach with Randy and Loren. It was getting a little warmer, so Michelle and I got some sun at the beach while Kim and Randy went hiking. Loren, after sniffing and observing everything in her radius, finally settled in for a nap under a shaded log, burrowing herself in the sand.

When Loren arose, we went for a brief walk around the beach. A stocky, tattooed guy, who was with his family and a handsome bulldog, looked over at us. I knew what was coming. The acknowledgement nod, something I experienced in high school whenever I saw another rocker type in the hallway. That almost imperceptible tilt of the chin, followed by slight knowing smile and a lift of the eyebrow.

"Nice dog," he said after the nod.

"Yours, too," I replied.

I get more attention with Loren than I ever did with Jake, my black lab. It's something of a status symbol, good or bad, to walk with a pit bull. A slight edge. Especially if you're a kind of secretary-ish white girl like me. Loren made me feel secure and cool at the same time, like, if I can handle this strong a dog, that somehow makes me tougher. God, in a small, sick way, did that logic put me on par with the gangbangers and bully breeders I disdained? Yikes.

Our last camping evening was spent grilling, cooking, and enjoying each other's offerings: mom's broccoli and chicken casserole with fresh baked rolls (can you see where I get this eating thing from?) and Michelle, Randy and

Kim's grilled steaks and squash. For dessert, Kim had brought along a double-sided flat iron to make what she called "chubbies."

"Rarely is food named after the effect it has on you," Randy observed sagely.

"For good reason," Michelle replied.

Recipe: Take two pieces of buttered bread and in between the unbuttered side of the slices layer apple, cherry, or a combination of both pie fillings, then squash together in the iron.

Hold the iron over an open flame until the buttered toast is crisp and the filling nice and hot (about six to eight minutes). Relinquish the chubby from its iron prison, then sprinkle with cinnamon sugar. Delish.

We worked off a bit of the evening's feast off on Sunday morning, when Michelle, Kim, Loren and I hiked a few miles near the bridge over Deception Pass, while my dad and Randy went fishing and Mom watched the camp. The earth was a deep reddish brown, surrounded by vines and lush trees, plants springing from every nook and cranny. Loren had a field day, investigating every bit of flora and fauna she could get her nose on.

Later on I read, my second favorite pastime on vacation (can you guess the first?). It was as peaceful as I'd felt in weeks, Loren laying at my feet as I lounged on a camping chair. She napped and I would watch her occasionally, a smile on my face, as her little white and pink chest moved and up down, a delicate snore escaping her snout. Things were winding down for both of us.

As we drove off the next morning, my parents and I stopped by the bridge over Deception Pass to take photos. High cliffs above ocean, the sound water blue and green, the woods lush, the sky expansive, the smell fresh and woodsy. We were there at the perfect time, too, a gorgeous summer day. My eyes took in as much as they could before we headed back to Mukilteo. We had a boat to catch.

***

Loren amazed me. We walked down the ramp on our way to Michelle and Randy's boat and the diva actually went over the metal gratings with nary a hesitation, even when the bridge swayed slightly to and fro. Probably because she was following Michelle's picnic basket, which contained fried clams, potato salad, and a host of other goodies.

When we came to their slip, I fretted about how to get Loren off the dock and into the boat, a 26-footer named Fishful Thinking. Randy just picked her up and gently placed her onto the decking, a very sweet gesture. For most of the short trip, Loren sat patiently by Randy's leg, a canine skipper to his captain. She wasn't startled by the engine or the water splashing up alongside the boat. Loren seemed as comfortable on a boat as she did in the car.

We cruised briefly around the Everett harbor. It was about 6:30 p.m. and the skies were clear. The sun was out, shimmering on the sea's surface. At one point, Loren looked skyward, closed her eyes, and took in a deep breath, as if committing the sights and sounds to memory.

"I'll be your skipper, Randy."

Unfortunately, high winds made the water choppy, so we quickly docked the boat back at Michelle and Randy's slip to eat.

The clams were tender and crisp under the cornmeal batter, as fresh as can be since Michelle and Randy had recently harvested them by hand on one of their many clamming trips. The Pacific Northwest life sure agrees with them and I found myself happy for my friend, if slightly envious. Besides the rain and gray skies which are pervasive most of the year, living here must be really cool.

Home

Our trek west took us through Seattle to Olympia and off to the 101, where we glimpsed a procession of former logging towns along the way. It's sad, these little towns, which probably once thrived but now just looked empty and downtrodden.

After many miles of forest, we turned a corner and caught a glimpse of the sea below, which was breathtaking. The Oregon coast looks much like Northern California, high, rugged cliffs with the sea crashing against them, then miles of sandy serenity, some cypresses appearing out of nowhere near the water.

Feeling a little decadent and very road-weary, I had upgraded us to a king oceanfront room with a fireplace at the Fireside Inn in Yachats so we could kick back and enjoy the view. It was well worth it.

The beach was layered with black, flat rocks surrounding the

"Hello? Anyone down there?"

shore, where waves crashed dramatically. The sound and the sights replenished my soul. The Fireside Inn was perfect for us and the many dog lovers that stayed here. Small dogs, big dogs, old dogs, they all enjoyed the endless trail that looped around ever-changing ocean views.

This part of the trip was about relaxing and winding down from our long adventure. I'd looked at the atlas with my father while camping and was shocked as we added up the states we had visited during our 50 days on the road. 29. That made Loren one very well-traveled dog and me one tired driver.

We went to Newport to view the Yaquina Bay lighthouse, which was set against the gorgeous Oregon coast, to take some pictures. Loren went pee under a sign that said public restrooms and I laughed. She is nothing if not polite. There was an awesome view of the Yaquina Bay Bridge, a long, beautiful stretch of steel highlighted by several gracefully curved arches, and I snapped away at the sight.

My mystery rash had reappeared and I suspected it might have something to do with my diet, shellfish perhaps, but when you're in one of the great seafood spots in the country, you gotta have it. For dinner that night, I ordered the Captain's Platter at Luna Sea in Yachats, a small storefront with the freshest fish around; the owner catches it on his boat from local waters. The grilled halibut, scallops, and shrimp were delicate and moist, spiced with just a little Cajun seasoning, and served up with hot crispy fries and refreshing coleslaw with sweet, tart bits of apples.

For breakfast the next day, we went to the Green Salmon, a funky, eco-friendly coffee shop swarming with local hippies. "The Green Salmon," a whole wheat bagel with Pacific Northwest lox, matcha or powdered tea cream cheese, ripe tomatoes, and piquant capers, caught my eye and it was a solid choice. We brought it back to our room, so we could enjoy the last of our oceanfront view before we headed off to Gold Beach, 172 miles away, for one night, then Petaluma before finally making it home. Loren stretched out across my feet on the bed as I alternately napped, read, or worked on the blog.

The next morning, we made a stop at the Green Salmon for provisions to go, this time a roasted mango cheese danish with toasted coconut. The danish had a thousand flaky, buttery layers surrounding the decadent, creamy center, with was also filled with bits of fresh, heady mango. Quite possibly the best pastry in the universe. If I ever went back to Yachats, I was going to beg their pastry chef for a lesson.

My plan was to take Loren to Cindy first, then head home. I was happy at the thought of getting back into my everyday routine, to cook in my own kitchen, to cuddle and play with my own dogs, to have my boyfriend's arms around me. This trip and being out of my element had been exciting, exhausting, intriguing, boring, fun, and scary. I had learned so much and met some incredible people who were doing so much to help the homeless animals in this country.

I'd also seen just how big the problem is, and it overwhelmed me. More than ever, I realized it's all about education and providing resources so that owners can find a way to keep their pet instead of dumping it at a shelter, where the most likely result is death.

My resolve to keep fighting on behalf of these animals was strengthened by what I'd seen, though I was more convinced than ever that the problem will never be solved completely, at least not in my lifetime. But as the saying goes, if you're not part of the solution, you're part of the problem.

***

We left Gold Beach, Oregon at 9 a.m., after taking a little walk along the shore. While not as scenic as the drive that preceded it, there were still some breathtaking rock formations in the ocean, partially covered by fog, before we entered the never-ending Redwood Highway. Loren seemed to like the cool, damp sand beneath her toes.

For hundreds of miles, we were surrounded by trees that reached heavenward. During the drive, I heard Daughtry's *Home* on the radio and started to cry, remembering all the people and places we'd encountered on this journey, as well as the family and friends whose support made the whole thing possible. It had been an incredible seven weeks and through it all, my faithful sidekick Loren had been just about impeccable. I reached back and petted her on the head as she snoozed, her head on the pillow in the cab. She, too, was going home.

"I love you, Boogie," I told her. "I'm gonna miss you, but you're going to have an awesome life with Cindy, your new mom. No more driving hundreds of miles every other day. You'll have your own place now, for good."

Her tawny eyes met mine briefly, imbued with their usual peaceful expression. Cindy had assured me I could visit Loren, which made me happy. I wanted to remain Loren's cool aunt Michelle, the one who took her on a wild trip across the country and continued to do fun things with her. I patterned this image after my own aunt GiGi, my mom's younger sister, who took me to the Hollywood Cemetery on her Vespa scooter when I was 10 because I was obsessed with old movie stars. A year later, she brought me to the Hare Krishna Festival at Venice Beach, which really blew my young mind.

The redwoods soon turned into golden rolling hills with sprawling oaks. It was hot, too, in the high 80s. No more coastal coolness. We were in Cali! There were medical marijuana billboards on the border to prove it. I grinned.

On the southbound 101, just past the Garberville exit, I spotted two creatures running up the highway. It was a small border collie and a cattle dog. I pulled over and called them to my truck. They came at once, panting in the harsh heat, happy to see a friendly human. They had collars, but no tags. If I see loose dogs in a residential area, I tend to leave them be, unless they have tags, so they can find their way home, rather than end up in a shelter. In this case, there were no homes within miles, just lots of hot asphalt.

The dogs jumped in the back of the truck with little encouragement and I poured them a big bowl of water, which they lapped up thirstily. Loren the diva watched the action from the air-conditioned cab, her ears at attention, looking at the new travelers with interest for a few seconds before settling back on her down pillow.

I got off the freeway and into town, where I found a side street and called Nancy.

"What do I do now?" I asked after telling her the situation.

"Call the police station or the fire station," she said. "Call 911."

My GPS gave me a phone number for the local sheriff station, but a voicemail answered, so I called 911.

"I found two stray dogs running up Highway 101," I said. "I need to talk to the Garberville police."

"Hey, thanks for the ride!"

I was connected to the sheriff's substation, which I found within a few minutes. Once at the station, after meeting the officers, I noticed that one of the collars had phone numbers embedded in it.

I left frantic messages on both voicemails and was assured that they would be safely held in a small, local shelter until the owners were found.

I kissed the little black and white dog goodbye on its head and wished them the best, hoping I had done the right thing. My phone rang two hours later. It was their owner, who was out of town. The dogs had been left with a friend and broke out of their backyard confinement. They were now staying with a different friend. Their owner was concerned because there was a third missing canine party, a large white female with black feet. I prayed the lost dog turned up soon, but felt good that this story had a mostly happy ending.

We stopped in Ukiah so I could get some cash and the friendly teller struck up a conversation with me after I said I had lost my ATM card.

"Did you get it in the mail yet?" he asked.

"No, I'm traveling and it should be there when I get home," I replied numbly.

"Really…where are you coming from?" he said.

For the life of me, I could not remember where we had spent the last night. Instead, I pulled out a postcard and rambled on about the overall road trip, that we were on our last day and heading back to Southern California tomorrow.

He took a look at our photo and was quiet for a minute.

"That looks just like my dog," he said. "We had to put him to sleep last year."

"Was he old?" I asked.

"No, he was only four, but he had lymphoma. He went from being 100 pounds to 60 pounds and couldn't function," he said. "It was the hardest day of my life."

"I'm so sorry," I said with sincere empathy. "I've had to put two of my dogs down and it was horrible. Two of the saddest days of my life."

The man gave me a half-smile. "Thank you," he said and held up the card. "Can I keep this?

"Yeah," I said.

"Be safe," he said as I left.

We arrived in Petaluma around 5:30 p.m., leaving me plenty of time for a 7 p.m. recovery meeting, which I desperately needed after going three weeks without, and to pick up dinner.

My last dinner on the road was an Asian shrimp salad from High-Tech Burrito in Petaluma, which I ate in the truck with Loren. Tasty, yes, but somewhat anticlimactic after all the amazing meals I'd had; I needed to eat something slightly healthy after my Oregon pig-out sessions.

In our room, Loren and I played with a makeshift woobie, a packet of Kleenex, to release some of her energy. Poor thing had been in the car most of the day. She ran back and forth from the door to the bathroom, tossing the pack up in the air. When I threw it on the bed, she jumped up and grabbed the pack, thrashing it around like a shark.

After a few minutes, Loren was over the woobie. She laid on the bed, a victorious smile on her face, having once again conquered the enemy.

Thankfully, Loren was in a snuggly mood on our last night. I held her close to me and whispered softly, "I am not going to cry tomorrow. It is going to be a happy day. You are meeting your new mom and you're going to have a wonderful life. No one deserves it more than you."

The tears started spilling down my face and onto Loren's fur. "Thank you for coming with me. I couldn't have had a better friend on this trip," I said. Loren let out a heavy sigh and lifted an arm for better belly-rubbing access. I obliged, happily.

Loren snored contentedly, but I didn't sleep much, worried about not waking up on time to deliver her to Cindy at 3 p.m. in Valencia. The 6:30 a.m. wake up call was a little startling, especially for a Saturday. I wasn't used to being on deadline anymore. We made our final Starbucks run before hitting the highway.

It was foggy and cold out in Petaluma. I covered Loren up with a shawl and braced myself for the 387 miles ahead. Though it was the 4th of July, traffic was light and the sun soon came out with a vengeance. This stretch of the 5 freeway reminded me of the Great Plains; flat, dry, seemingly never-ending, with a few gas stations, hotels, and chain restaurants every 30 to 50 miles to remind you that you were still in civilization. Loren slept up front almost the whole way home, allowing me access to pat her sleek body throughout the trip.

We pulled up in Valencia a little early, at 2:20 p.m. I stopped the car and sighed. It truly was Independence Day for Loren. She sat up and looked around, then back at me, ready for the latest adventure. I gave her a final kiss on the forehead and looked her deep in the eyes.

"Don't say I never took you anywhere," I said with a laugh. Loren licked me on the nose in response, my sweet kissy-poo. Oh, how I was going to miss her.

I got out of the car and opened Loren's door. She jumped out and we headed up the driveway. My heart pounded as I knocked on the front door. Loren seemed excited, too. She was probably as sick of driving as I was and ready for a change of pace.

"This is it," I said to her with a nervous grin.

Cindy opened the door and welcomed Loren.

"Hi pretty girl," she said. "Come on in."

Loren did just that, acting as if she owned the place, running about and sniffing the rooms with carefree abandon, her tail whipping around at 60 miles per hour. Cindy's friend Chris was there to meet Loren, too, and we all went outside briefly to look at the backyard and give Loren some cool water. Cindy was indeed a solid woman, about 5' 5" and probably 160 or 170 pounds. She looked strong enough to handle Loren.

When we went inside, Loren ran from the couch to the ground, snuggling up with Chris for a few minutes, then hopping back on the couch with Cindy.

"Wow, she really is a sweetie. I thought my dog was sweet, but she's even more so. Wanna trade?" Chris asked jokingly.

"No way," Cindy said, hugging Loren tight.

Cindy showed me the rest of the house. Most of it was tiled, which she said her former dogs loved to lay on in the summertime; I imagined Loren would, too. There were pictures of them, a beautiful Rottweiler and a striking black pit/Lab mix, both girls.

Cindy then pulled out a beautiful, round tapestry dog bed and a huge woobie she had bought for Loren. Perhaps I had been too judgmental.

The doorbell rang. It was Nancy, who was picking Loren up for a few days so she could have her bathed and get her paperwork in order before being delivered to Cindy for good the following Tuesday. Loren jumped on Nancy and hugged her legs for more than a few seconds.

"Lo, Lo, Lorenzo," Nancy called out, hugging her right back, a broad smile breaking out on her usually serious face.

Nancy is my hero. She saved Loren from the shelter two and a half years prior and had taken care of her ever since, along with 90 other dogs. Loren owed her life to Nancy and it seemed she knew it.

Loren tore herself away from Nancy and jumped right back on the couch with Cindy, who wrapped an arm around her. They looked very content together. I relaxed and decided to be truly happy about the adoption.

"Thank you for adopting her," I said to Cindy, then turned to Loren and gave her a final kiss on the forehead. "Bye, Loren. Have a great life."

Loren gave me a kiss and looked from me to Cindy quizzically for a second, but stayed put on the couch. I waved goodbye and smiled. The tile led me to the front door and I made my way into the blistering Santa Clarita Valley heat. Once in the truck, I let out a deep breath, but no tears. This was a happy ending, after all.

I unplugged Gidget with a flourish. Home. I knew the route.

Third Time's a Charm

It took me an hour to get home from Valencia and I enjoyed the drive way more than I usually did, taking the time to really see where I lived. I made the turn from the off ramp and followed the ten miles of two-lane highway that leads to Mt. Pinos or Pine Mountain Club by way of Frazier Park. Situated in the Los Padres Forest, the dense packs of pine trees poked their way heavenwards from both sides of the mountain range, just like I remembered them.

Pastoral ranches on rolling hills, with cows grazing in the fields, filled my vision before I made the turn onto the two-lane highway that has about five miles of mild twists and turns before the small town of Pine Mountain Club becomes apparent, first from the cabin-style houses, then from the golf course, club house, and village area, which is home to restaurants, a general store, real estate offices, and gift shops. I rolled down my window and breathed in the clean air. After all the places I'd seen in America, I was happy to realize that my hometown was one of the prettiest.

Wayde was home and greeted me with a big hug. We stood there for a few minutes, rocking quietly back and forth

"Welcome back," he said, holding me at arm's length and smiling at me all the way from his brown eyes to his full lips, which are surrounded by a lush brown goatee.

"Good to be back," I said, with a big sigh, collapsing into his firm chest and snuggling closer.

Wayde took my hand and led me around the newly remodeled second floor of our home.

There were wall-to-wall oak hardwood floors, a center island in the kitchen and a cast-iron wood stove, standing before a custom stone wall, in the living room. It was gorgeous. My BF did good work.

We went downstairs to see Buster and Sam, who were definitely excited that mama was home. Their wiggling butts and dancing tails went into overdrive. So much so, that they turned on each other and fought. It was time, after all, for their annual "who is the alpha male?" scuffle. Buster always loses, but never fails to give it the college try. Wayde, apparently the new alpha in our pack, broke it up within 30 seconds.

Life went back to normal the next week. I was back at the paper and excited about writing the latest installment of our saga, which was going to focus on Loren's new life with Cindy. The Sunday after her delivery, I had just updated the blog with a cutesy post in Loren's voice, saying how happy she was, complete with touching photos of the happy new family, including shots of her with Cindy's ten-year old grandson. I had visited with them all on Wednesday and everyone seemed really thrilled to be together.

Within 20 minutes of posting it, I received an email from Nancy with the subject line "Loren got returned." My heart dropped. What happened? I clicked on the email with dread. Cindy had left Loren alone to run an errand and she had destroyed some custom window blinds and the windowsill in a fit of separation anxiety.

I called Nancy. "Oh my God," I said, holding tears back.

"Yeah," Nancy sighed. "It sucks."

"I just can't believe it…" I trailed off.

"Well, I told Cindy that we could provide her with a trainer to learn how to crate train Loren," Nancy said.

"Did she seem interested?" I asked hopefully, trying not to blubber like a baby.

"Yes. I'm going to put in a few calls and see what we can arrange," Nancy replied.

She was in efficiency mode, while I was a trembling wreck. Nancy had more than 20 years in rescue, so her skin was a lot thicker than mine. I don't know how she dealt with it, people dumping dogs, returning dogs, mistreating dogs. Nancy saw the worst of mankind on a daily basis and still stayed sane, if a little gruff.

"Can I call Cindy? I need to know what to do about my story," I said.

"Go ahead. Just give it a day or two," Nancy said. "Meanwhile, I'll find her a trainer and a crate."

On Tuesday, the day before my deadline, I called Cindy. I asked her what happened and Cindy told me about the destruction, Loren's anxiety, and how sad she was because otherwise, Loren was a really good dog.

"I thought you were going to look at crate training her?" I asked.

"Well," came the whiny response. "I was, but you know, I can't take her over to my neighbors who have dogs because she doesn't get along with them."

"You could just leave her in the crate when you go visit them," I responded. "Or invite them over to your house without their dogs."

"Well, everyone's kind of afraid of her," she said. "Because she's a pit bull."

"Actually, she's a Staffordshire/bulldog mix, but you know Loren. She's very sweet. They just need to get to know her," I said.

There was a pause for a moment.

"Oh, but then what about when I go away for a weekend? I wanted to take her with me, but if she doesn't like other dogs, then…" Cindy's voice trailed off.

"You could hire a dog sitter. I could stay with her," I responded.

"My neighbors say she whines whenever I leave her in the backyard. It's just so hard..." she trailed off again.

Sick of her excuses, I began to lose patience.

"Look Cindy, there's a solution to every one of the issues you presented. The bottom line is, if Loren's not the right dog for you, then just say so," I said, trying to keep a low, even tone.

Silence.

"Well, I guess she's not. She's really sweet, but I just can't deal with her problems," Cindy said.

My face flooded with red hot anger, followed by a wave of incredible despair. "Alright. Thank you," was all I could make out before hanging up my cell phone.

I was in at work, in the former photo room, a black and grey windowless expanse the staff had dubbed "The Dungeon." Sobs racked my body. I lay my head down in my folded arms on the scratched wooden table. I sat there for a few minutes, trying to compose myself before re-entering the newsroom, which was an open bull pen. I was too devastated to be embarrassed.

I wiped my nose on my sleeve and headed back to my desk, head hanging low. Michele, my boss, took one look at my face and stood up to give me a hug.

"What happened?" she asked.

"Loren got returned..." I said and sobbed into her shoulder.

Michele handed me a napkin from her desk so I could blot away the tears. "Oh, I'm so sorry," she said, frowning. "That just sucks."

It did, indeed. I felt like I had failed Loren somehow. Instead of the happy ending I had hoped to write, *The Signal* ran an adoption plea for Loren, complete with what I thought was her cutest photo from the trip. There were no takers.

When I went to The Brittany Foundation to volunteer the following Saturday, Loren ran about her kennel excitedly, launching herself off one end to the other. Her tongue was hanging out. It was a hot summer day in the Southern California desert. I walked straight into her kennel, ignoring the barks of the twelve other dogs, and sat on top of her Igloo. She hugged my legs and wiped drool all over my shirt before lapping my face with a big, wet kiss.

"Oh, Booger," I said. "I'm so sorry. I was hoping this was it for you."

Weeks turned into months and then it was fall, time for Bow-Wows & Meows annual pet fair, which occurs the second Sunday of every October. I had gotten involved with the non-profit organization after covering the event for the paper three years prior and had become a board member, as well as its public relations director and raffle coordinator.

I'm proud to count Yvonne Allbee, the fair's founder, among my closest friends. Inspired by the love of her rescued dog Bear and cat Sam, Yvonne began Bow-Wows & Meows in 2000 with the hope of educating the public about the homeless pet problem and encouraging adoption. It grew from a small event with a few vendors and homeless animals to a full-fledged fair, complete with more than 60 booths, adoptable pets from six Los Angeles County shelters, a live DJ, animal-related entertainment, and a fun dog show with ten categories. Many rescue organizations and advocacy groups also participate.

Bow-Wows & Meows is free, festive, and the only adoption fair in The Santa Clarita Valley. In 2008, we adopted out 125 animals, yet Yvonne and I cried in the parking lot over the few dogs and cats that went back in the animal control trucks, the ones who didn't find a home that day.

For the 2009 fair, Yvonne had a special bright pink banner made for Loren with some of her best photos and text that read "Loren, Pit Bull Celebrity. Loves ice cream, belly rubs, and is sweeter than sweet. Pit bull ambassador that traveled the country." She was inspired by Loren's Facebook fan page of the same name, which had already amassed 300 friends, mostly people that knew us or had read about our journey. Yvonne, always my biggest cheerleader, was now doing all she could for Loren, too. It touched me.

We hung the banner in The Brittany Foundation booth, which was being manned by April Lund, a new and incredibly passionate volunteer, and several others. Around noon, when the fair was in full swing, April came over to me at the raffle table, which had over 50 prizes available and was always bustling.

"Michelle, you have to meet this family. They're really interested in Loren," April said.

I took a deep breath. "Really?" I asked.

"Really. They just seem to love her. I'm bringing them over right now. Stay put," April said, dashing through the crowds to retrieve Loren and her potential adopters.

Within minutes, a nice-looking couple in their mid-thirties, trailed by three young daughters, came over, the dad holding Loren's leash in his hand. April stood behind them and beamed.

Loren, who was outfitted in a bright pink knit bandana, stood at the dad's feet and calmly accepted the affection being lavished on her by the three girls, the youngest of which appeared to be four and the oldest about ten. The mom bent down and petted Loren on her head.

"Loren seems really sweet," the dad said. "Can you tell me more about her?"

"Well, she and I traveled 29 states in 50 days and she was a great am-bassador for her breed. Loren loves kids, she can sleep in for up to ten hours without a break, she doesn't require much exercise," I said. "Oh, she loves to go for car rides and likes vanilla ice cream, too."

The dad smiled.

"Mostly, Loren just likes being around people," I said. "She's the most people-centric dog I've ever met."

"Sure seems that way," the dad said, looking down fondly at Loren. April was giving me the thumbs up sign behind him as we talked. I shook my head and rolled my eyes at her.

"Have you ever had a bully breed before?" I asked.

"Well, we had a boxer about the same size," he said.

"Do you have any problems with owning a pit bull?" I asked. "Loren's really a Staffordshire/bulldog mix, but everyone thinks she's a pit bull when they see her."

The mom had stood up and joined her husband by then.

"No, we don't have a problem with Loren's breed," she said. "As long as she's good with the kids, which she sure seems to be."

"I have to tell you, Loren has separation anxiety and needs to be in a crate when you leave the house," I said.

The couple looked at each other. "Well, I work from home and my wife is a stay-at-home mom, so she wouldn't be left alone much," the dad said.

OMG. They did seem to be the perfect family. "Sounds great. If you're really interested, April will give you an application," I said, shaking their hands. "I have to get back to the raffle." I bent down and pet Loren, who loved being the center of attention. She gave me a quick lick before returning to her young audience.

April led the family back to the Brittany Foundation booth. She came over an hour later and told me that the family had toured the fair, then returned to see Loren one more time. The dad had called her "my dog" and assured April they would fax their application that night.

"I think this is the family God wanted for her," April, who is a born again Christian, said to me. "I have a really good feeling about it."

My lip started trembling. I tried to hold it in, but couldn't. "You really think so?" I asked tearily.

April nodded and hugged me. "This is it, Michelle. I feel it." I went limp in April's arms and sobbed, then pulled away, wiping back tears and smiling. She gave me an empathetic smile before vanishing into the crowd.

The family never called, never faxed, never emailed about Loren. I played out the most likely scenario in my head: they went home, told their friends and family about wanting to adopt a pit bull and promptly got talked out of it. It burned me, but I tried to think of the positive. Bow-Wows & Meows had broken its adoption record, finding homes for 165 dogs and cats by the end of the five-hour fair. Loren still had The Brittany Foundation to return to, the shelter animals didn't. It was much more urgent for them to find a family.

Right before Christmas, The Brittany Foundation was invited to be the recipient for Whole Foods Market Valencia's annual Heart of the Holidays event. Shoppers would be asked to contribute an item off our wish list and we could bring adoptable dogs to showcase in our outdoor booth. Margo's Bark Root Beer would be there, too.

It was great to see Tim and Jessica Youd again. They started Margo's Bark after creating a root beer for their son Oscar's science fair project. The brew was so good, the Youds decided to bottle it and named it after their rescue dog Margo. One hundred percent of the profits from Margo's Bark benefits shelters and rescues, such as The Brittany Foundation, and the Youds have been directly responsible for saving many a canine life by pledging to donate hundreds of dollars toward the rescue of death row dogs at shelters.

The day before Heart of the Holidays, Nancy had received an email from a family with two young sons and no other pets that was interested in Loren. They were going to meet her during the event, so I was cautiously hopeful that Loren would get the best Christmas present of all, a new home.

When a Hispanic couple in their mid-to-late twenties with two small boys approached the booth and set their gaze on Loren, I knew it was them. I walked over and introduced us. The dad, Eddie, was tall, with a shaved head. He wore a blue Dodgers t-shirt and had very kind brown eyes. He bent down and looked at Loren, then smiled when she gave him a big sloppy kiss.

"Hello, girl," Eddie said. She kissed him again and he laughed. "You are a sweetheart, huh?"

The boys, who were about three and six, petted Loren along with their father, but soon became distracted by the activity around the booth. Their mom, Miriam, kept a close eye on them as they visited with some of the smaller dogs we had in little pens under the canopy.

"So, you're interested in Loren? How come?" I asked her.

"I just fell in love with her picture. She looked so sweet and it said she's good with kids," Miriam said.

"She is," I assured her. "When we were on the road this summer, Loren was great with all the little kids that came over to pet her, and some were as young as two."

I handed Eddie Loren's leash and we took a walk around the parking lot. Loren wasn't acting too stubborn this time, but quickly decided to take a break under a tree on the grass near the sidewalk. Eddie laughed and sat down beside her. The boys came over and gave her a pet, too. The whole family's vibe was very mellow. I imagined Loren sitting on the couch with them, watching Dodger games and being fed bits of hot dog.

I explained Loren's separation anxiety, her need to be crate trained and to stay away from close contact with other dogs, but that otherwise, she was a really good girl. Miriam, a stay at home mom, assured me Loren would get lots of attention. She told me Eddie had wanted to adopt a three-legged Rottweiler named Max from the shelter and was disappointed when someone else beat him to it. That warmed my heart. Anyone that could fall in love with a tripod "dangerous breed" dog was alright in my book. They also owned their own townhome, which according to them, didn't have any breed restrictions.

One thing concerned me, though. The family had adopted a young boxer/pit bull mix earlier that year, but returned him because their neighbor complained about his whining, plus he was hyper and would knock down the kids. I explained to Miriam that Loren might whine at first, but should settle down once she got used to a routine.

On my way home, I relayed that information to Nancy as she went over Loren's adoption application, which the family had filled out at the event.

"Other than that, I liked them. Again, not who I imagined Loren to be with, but I'd give them a B," I said.

"Alright, well, I'll take a B," Nancy said.

Nancy asked the family about what happened with the previous dog and was told they had found a no-kill rescue to bring him to. We decided to give them the benefit of the doubt, as everything else checked out OK.

Loren was delivered to Eddie and Miriam's small Canyon Country townhome three days before Christmas. It made my holidays bright, knowing Loren was with a family instead of in the kennels, which were soon to be hit by cold, rainy winter weather.

They were fostering her first to make sure it was a fit, but assured Nancy that adoption would be imminent if everything worked out.

I was allowed to visit Loren after a few weeks so I could take photos and get info for the blog. Loren seemed really happy, running with a big, goofy grin on her face. She jumped on the couch for a family portrait, laying her head on Eddie's lap as he laughed. The townhome was tiny and spare, but it was much better than the kennel Loren was used to. The family was taking the time to crate train her, too, with professional help we provided through Danielle Haffner of Dog Works Training.

By the beginning of February, the family had bad news. Eddie had been laid off from his job as a teaching assistant and they were struggling. They didn't think they could keep Loren. Since they were a foster family, Nancy and I assured them that we would provide food and medical attention for Loren, if necessary, until they got back on their feet and adopted her. I even took up a small collection from friends and presented it to them, to help make ends meet. They were very grateful.

In mid-February, the same neighbor who complained about their previous dog had left a note threatening to "take their stupid dog to the pound" if "it didn't stop whining." A week or so later, Eddie and Miriam's homeowners association sent out a notice that the liability insurance company had required that "no dangerous breed dogs be allowed in the common areas." Nancy and I put Talitha or Tally, our new volunteer who just happened to have passed the bar exam that month, on the case. Tally issued stern warnings to both the neighbor and the HOA about the family's rights. Neither were heard from again.

During a lunchtime visit I made to Loren in early March, Miriam revealed that the family was five months behind in their mortgage payments and that the bank wouldn't work with them on a modification, so they would either have to foreclose or possibly do a short sale. My heart dropped.

"What about Loren?" I asked.

"Well, we'll keep her if we can. It might be hard to find a rental that will take her, but we'll try," Miriam said. I told her I would do anything I could to help.

As I drove back to work, I thought about it. Five months behind would have put them at missing their first mortgage payment in October or November. What were they thinking about, taking in a dog during such chaos? I sighed and hoped for the best, but had a sinking suspicion that Loren's days with this family were numbered.

Toward the end of March, as I walked with Buster around Pine Mountain Club, a random thought popped into my head. "Well, if Loren gets returned, at least she had a nice, cozy home to live in during winter." When I got home and checked my Yahoo account that morning, sure enough, there was an email from the family that they were returning Loren because finances forced them to move in with Miriam's mother and her apartment building didn't accept pets. They were taking Loren back to The Brittany Foundation later on that week.

I shook my head. I knew it. I let out a big sigh and my eyes teared up, but it was much less painful than when Cindy returned Loren for some reason. Maybe my skin was beginning to thicken or maybe I had just realized that I didn't have control over Loren's life. As my friend Liz liked to remind me, "That dog has a higher power and it's not you." If Loren were a shelter dog facing death, it would be totally different. I knew she always had a safe place to return to.

In a selfish way, it was nice to have Loren back at The Brittany Foundation. It hadn't been the same there without her. I loved seeing her silly face, getting the kisses, and bonding in Dogway, especially since Buffy, my second favorite dog at the rescue and the most affectionate behind Loren, had been adopted by Kelly, a long-time volunteer, in January.

I remained hopeful for Loren, but realized she wasn't unhappy at Brittany. As a matter of fact, when we returned from a research trip to Best Friends in November, her ears perked up and her tail started wagging as soon as we pulled into the rescue's parking lot. Then she dragged me back to her kennel and very calmly settled in. This was the home Loren had known for three years, after all. Still, I harbored fantasies that one day, the right person would claim Loren as their own.

In late March, Nancy received an email from a 26-year old man in Studio City who was interested in a pit bull puppy we had listed, a female being fostered in Little Rock. His name was Stefan Niemczyk and he wanted to rescue a pit bull because he felt they were great dogs and had a bad rap. Nancy was concerned about Stefan's ability to raise a puppy with his erratic hours as a private chef, plus his apartment had no yard. We knew that the puppy he was interested in would grow to be huge, too, at least 80 pounds.

Nancy asked Stefan if he would possibly be interested in an older dog, one that was already crate trained. If so, she suggested he come and meet Loren, which he did on April 11. He drove a shiny black 300Z and emerged from the car, tall, dark-haired and muscular, with a very sweet smile and bright blue eyes.

"Are you Michelle?" he asked as I made my way through the kennel door to greet him.

"Yes, Stefan?" I asked.

"Yes," he said and shook my hand.

"Did you find us OK?" I asked.

"Yep, no problem."

"Great. Let's go meet Loren," I said.

I introduced Stefan to all the big dogs before we came back to Loren. We entered her kennel and Loren immediately hugged his legs, stretching upwards for a kiss.

"Hi girl," he said softly, scratching under her velvet chin.

Loren sat and calmly accepted his attention, eyes closed, opening them every so often to peek at Stefan and give him a kiss. She rolled over on her back and showed Stefan her belly, which he rubbed with affection.

"What a sweet girl," he said, a wide grin playing out across his face.

"Let's take her for a walk," I said, handing him the leash. Loren dragged Stefan through the kennel area and waited by his car, ready for a road trip. He laughed.

"You think we're going for a ride, girl?" he asked.

"That's what she's hoping, anyway," I said. "Come on, Loren."

Loren moved a few feet, then dug her heels in and laid down. I sighed. Well, if Stefan was interested in Loren, it was better that he saw her quirks up front. "Come on, girl," he said, patiently, tugging at the leash gently. "Let's go."

Surprisingly, Loren got right up and once we got around the bend, became enthusiastic about the walk.

"She's good on a leash," Stefan commented. We got about a quarter mile up the dirt road when Loren decided to do her business. Stefan smiled.

"Good girl," he said.

We walked on and chatted. I told him about our trip and Loren's challenges in finding a home. Stefan told me that he was from Philadelphia, had grown up with big dogs, but hadn't had a dog of his own since moving out. He loved pit bulls and wanted to give one a good home, especially since he knew that many were treated badly.

"It breaks my heart. They're such good dogs," he said, bending over to pet Loren, who stopped. "Aren't you?" he asked. She licked his nose and he laughed.

"Is this my new daddy? For real?"

Back at the ranch, I had Stefan sit on the porch with Loren for a few minutes. Nancy had just returned from an appointment and wanted to talk with him after finishing up a chore. I figured it would give them time to bond.

I went back to cleaning kennels, sneaking a peek at the duo. Loren had her head in his lap and Stefan was talking to her, scratching behind her ears. They looked very cozy. When Nancy joined them a minute later, I focused on sweeping and raking the pea gravel, saying a little prayer for Loren.

"Please, please, let Stefan be Loren's daddy," I said, closing my eyes and adding, "If it's meant to be."

A few minutes later, I saw Stefan heading for the kennel door. I let him in and led them both back to Loren's kennel, closing the door behind us. He slipped the soft pink cloth choke collar off Loren's neck and bent down to her level.

"So what do you think?" I asked.

He looked into her eyes and then at me. "Loren's great. I love her demeanor," he replied, looking back at Loren, whose head was in his hands. "I have to be honest. I've been looking at rescues and shelters since I put in the adoption application with you, but I haven't met any dogs with Loren's personality. She's just so calm and sweet."

"She's the best," I agreed, then paused. "So…do you want her?"

"Yes," he said, nodding, looking back at Loren. "I do. Loren's the dog for me."

"Yeah!" I said. "That's awesome."

He gave Loren a final kiss. "Bye, girl," he said.

We walked back to his car and Stefan looked pensive. "I just have a lot going on right now. I'm auditioning for a Food Network show and have to travel quite a bit over the next few weeks," Stefan said. "I won't be ready to take Loren until May, if that's OK."

"That's fine," I told him. "Loren and I are scheduled for one more road trip, to finish up research for the book. We'll be back on May 3."

"Cool. Let me look at my schedule. I'll give Nancy a call and we'll set up the home check and delivery date," Stefan said. He looked back at Loren's kennel and waved at her.

"So, Stefan…" I said. "Can I be happy about this? Honestly?"

Stefan paused for a second and looked straight into my eyes. "Yes," he said. "You can be happy about this."

***

On May 16, I drove Loren down to Studio City and Stefan's apartment. She lounged in the back of the cab, her eyelids growing droopier with every passing mile. I reached back and rubbed her belly, silently communicating all the hopes I had for her and Stefan.

Stefan lived in a nice new three-story building, painted in Mediterranean tones. While it was located at the heart of a busy intersection, there was a park right across the street. We pulled up next to the park and Stefan came out to meet us. I let Loren out of the truck and her tail started wagging when she saw him.

"Hi girl," he said excitedly. "How are you?" He bent down to give Loren a hug, then stood up and gave me one, too. I handed him the leash and we went for a walk around the park. Stefan's grin was huge as he watched Loren sniff around.

"What do you think, girl? You like it here?" he asked, beaming like a proud parent.

"That's so cool that you have a park right across the street," I said.

"Yeah, it's perfect, huh?" Stefan said, then looked wistfully at his new dog. "I figure this is where we'll go for walks and to go potty, Lolo."

Wow. He already had a nickname for her. This was a good sign.

I handed Stefan a roll of poop bags, which were encased in a cloth cheetah. "It's always considerate to pick up the poop. You don't have to keep the cheetah," I said with a laugh.

"Naw, it's cute," Stefan replied, taking it from me, though his eyes were fixed on Loren. "My mom, who's my best friend, was worried about me getting a dog, since I'm so busy and all, but I explained to her that I was ready for this. Of course, she was also a little concerned because Loren is a bully breed. But I showed her the picture you sent me, of Loren on the bed with the little bow around her neck, and she just melted."

I smiled. I had kept in touch with Stefan over the last month, emailing crate-training tips along with the most adorable photos of Loren saying, "Hi daddy. I can't wait to see you!" I knew resistance would be futile.

"What about your apartment manager? Was she cool with Loren?" Stefan's apartment had a no pit bull policy.

"Yeah, I showed her Loren's DNA papers and it was no problem," he said.

The three of us stopped in front of the building. "Are you ready to see your new home, Loren?" Stefan asked.

We walked up the stairs to the glass door. Stefan punched a code and Loren trotted right in, to his delight. "You go on in, girl," he said.

The marble-filled lobby and rich carpeted hallway made the building seem more like a hotel than an apartment. I was impressed. Stefan's apartment was on the first floor and decorated in neutral shades of taupe and white. Black accessories included a huge entertainment center with a plasma flat screen TV and a long leather couch. A laptop was perched on its sidearm. From appearances, Stefan was doing pretty well.

"It's small, but I figure it's big enough for both of us, huh, girl?" he said to Loren.

To me, he said, "Please make yourself comfortable. I'll go and get the crate out of your truck." First, he brought me a glass of water. Stefan was a real gentleman.

While Stefan was out, Loren sniffed the perimeter. Satisfied after only a few minutes, she walked to the couch and promptly laid on her side right next to it. Loren let out a heavy sigh and closed her eyes. I laughed.

Stefan came back in with the crate, which he laid down next to Loren's brand new fleece dog bed, topped with a huge rawhide bone. Loren got up and greeted him.

"You should have seen her, Stefan," I said. "She passed out right by your couch within five minutes."

"Oh, that's good girl," he said,

"Yes, this will do nicely."

holding her face up to his. "I'm glad you feel at home here. I think we're a perfect match."

She sniffed his shirt, his biceps, then kissed his face as he grinned. They walked over to the fridge, where Stefan pulled a bag out.

"My friend, who's a chef, made you some organic dog treats," he told Loren as he dug into the bag. "I hope they're not too fancy for you."

She took the treat gently from his hand and crunched it happily. "Oh, good girl, I'm glad you like them," he said, rubbing her head and smiling.

I put my hand to my heart. I was dying of cuteness. This buff young man and the buff bully girl were falling in love, right before my eyes.

"I figure we'll make dinner together tonight," he told Loren, who gazed up adoringly at him. "Then my girlfriend's coming over. She loves dogs, too."

I took a final sip of water and stood up. "I'm gonna go," I said. "Here's Loren's file and vet information, as well as the contact info for the trainer, if you need her. You seem perfectly fine here."

Stefan gave me a solid bear hug.

"Can I visit once in a while?" I asked.

"Are you kidding? I feel like we adopted her together, after all you two have been through," he said. "You're family now. I'll be sending you updates, don't worry. You can call or come by any time."

I patted Loren on the head and kissed her right between the eyes. She licked me goodbye and Stefan bent down to hug her.

"You are a lucky girl," I said. "Be good."

Loren cocked her head slightly and looked at me, but didn't make a motion to move. Instead, she nestled closer into Stefan's broad chest.

"Do you want me to show you out?" Stefan asked.

"No, I'm fine," I said, determined to make it to the front door without looking back. "You two be happy."

The carpeted tunnel led me into the sunlight and I opened the glass door. Once in the truck, I clasped my hands in the prayer position and held them to my face for a minute. Not sure whether to laugh or cry, I did a little bit of both. Mostly, I just felt warm inside.

One year, one day, and more than 10,000 miles from the start of our journey, Loren was finally at home. Maybe I was being Pollyana-ish again, but I didn't care. Something in my gut told me Stefan was truly Loren's forever person. He was what I dreamt for her all along. Maybe sometimes the best really is saved for last.

I remembered something Stacey at Animal Farm Foundation had said to me, about how she liked to make sure her dogs got to go out to play and sniff and walk around every day, so that they would have good dreams at night. I hoped some of our crazy adventures would find their way into Loren's dreams as she made new memories with Stefan.

There was a new pit bull at The Brittany Foundation, a one-year old black and white male with a huge head and even bigger smile. His name was Jake. He needed a little training since he was so awkward and massive, but he was really coming along and stealing volunteer hearts with every passing day. I wondered how Jake would do on the road.

Turning the key, I smiled to myself. One dog at a time.

"Hi Daddy...good to be home...hope you like bully kisses...because I am the queen!"

Epilogue

Loren and Stefan continue to be a perfect match. He cooks her mini burgers and posts pictures of his Lolo, including one of her in a chef's hat, on Facebook. Stefan's kind girlfriend, Marlyse Phlaum, has stepped up as the most important woman in Loren's life. Together, they are not only training Loren to get along with Marlyse's dogs, Bella and

Marlyse, Loren and Stefan, one cool California family

Lola, but are taking her on runs up to four miles long. Aunt Michelle is always welcome to visit.

The deaf white pit bull puppy in New Orleans was renamed Bijoux and adopted within weeks after we met Ken Foster, who personally delivered her to a family in Baltimore.

At ARNO, Carrollton and all her pups were adopted, as were Brenna, Maverick and Arby. Grateful was sent to a top pit bull training rescue in Boston. Little Red still awaits her forever home. Buzz Lightyear didn't make it more than a few days after our departure. Jackson, Carrollton's boyfriend, also passed away from Addison's disease.

Deuce from Bama Bully Rescue was officially adopted by April and Tony Durden in June 2010. His handsome face can be found on Bama Bully t-shirts that proclaim "Blame the deed, not the breed." Bama Bully Shirts are available online at CafePress.com.

Benson, Scarface, Punky, and Bear from Animal Farm Foundation have all been adopted into loving homes; Benson is a service dog for a single mother with multiple sclerosis.

Daisy Faelten Balawejder of Hello Bully went to Missouri in July 2009 to help with rescue efforts after the largest federal dog-fighting bust to date, which resulted in more than 500 dogs looking for homes. Daisy took Kolby, a fawn and white bully with huge pointy ears, back to Pittsburgh and into the Hello Bully fold. He was adopted in February 2010. Since its inception, Hello Bully's Pit Fix Plus spay/neuter/vaccination program has helped more than 700 Pittsburgh bullies and their families.

Susie Gilbert left her job at WPHS and is once again working as a support group counselor. She volunteers at WPHS as a bully breed trainer.

Christelle Del Prete lost her beloved Dachsund, Simon, in February 2010. She only lasted three days before adopting two more dogs, Dutchess the dachsund and Dora the Australian shepherd/border collie, in Simon's honor.

My cousin Eddy Maxwell adopted kitten littermates Surprise and Santo in the summer of 2009, which helped cushion the blow when she lost her sweet Simon in March 2010.

Nina Gaither of Indy Humane said goodbye to her beautiful pit bull Lex in February 2010. Lex was a Canine Good Citizen, a Search and Rescue Dog, and a true ambassador for his breed.

Kathleen Mannix of ResQ Awearness has relocated to California and is now a dog trainer at Linda Blair's Worldheart Foundation in Acton, CA. She rescued a male pit bull puppy named Zuke and brings him with her to work.

Many of the big Brittany Foundation dogs found homes; in addition to Buffy, Doza was adopted and Kirby the Terrier is now in foster care with our volunteer Gina Tucci. Miley Cyrus the Yorkie was adopted by a family with young children; she has been renamed Ginger.

The Brittany Foundation turned a corner in November 2009 with our inaugural "Day In Their Paws" annual fundraiser. Volunteers spent up to 24 hours in a kennel with the dog of their choice to illustrate how shelter dogs live every day. Sponsors bought our freedom for $1 per minute; we raised more than $20,000. Legendary heavy metal singer Ronnie James Dio made an appearance at the event to free his wife Wendy from her kennel and sign autographs. He was a beautiful person and I'm very grateful I got to meet him before he passed away in May 2010.

I had an agent for *Pit Stops* in 2009, then got summarily dumped in the new year when she didn't find this book to be "enough of a life-changing journey" and that my "writing just wasn't there." I almost gave up but then I saw a movie called *The Runaways*. At the end, it tells how Joan Jett, whom I revere, released *I Love Rock N' Roll* after getting rejected by 28 different record labels. The album sold 10 million copies and she was the first woman to start her own record label. Inspired, I started my own publishing company, Say The Words Press. The result is in your hands.

Me, Wayde and our four-legged pack are still happy and healthy in the mountains. Sam and Buster have remained scuffle-free for over a year now. Sugar Butt is still a princess.

Resource Directory

There are many ways you can help homeless pets:

- Always adopt from a shelter or rescue and encourage your friends and family to do so, as well.
- If you can't adopt, consider fostering an animal temporarily until they find a home. Most rescues will pay the food and medical costs while a foster pet is in your care.
- Spay and neuter your pets.
- Volunteer at your local rescue or shelter. Volunteering can include everything from cleaning kennels and walking dogs to helping out at fundraising/adoption events to grant writing, public relations or website development.
- Donate to your local rescue or shelter, which are always in need of funds and items such as dog food, treats, toys, and blankets.
- If you like to drive, offer to transport for your local rescue, which often pull dogs from shelters in other counties or even across the state or the country.

To find an adoptable pet or a shelter or rescue in your community, visit:

www.adoptapet.com
www.petfinder.com

Pit Bull Rescue Central is a nationwide online directory that offers advice on everything from what to do if you find a stray pit bull to how to host private party pit bull adoptions or find an adoptable pit bull in your community. www.pbrc.net

If you suspect someone in your community is involved in dog fighting, report them to the Humane Society of the United States dog fighting hotline at (877) 847-4787. A reward of $5,000 is offered for information leading to the arrest and conviction of a dogfighter. All information is kept confidential.

Rescues, Shelters and Advocacy Groups by State

Alabama
Bama Bully Rescue
P.O. Box 241002
Montgomery, AL 36124
www.bamabully.org
mail@bamabully.org

Mobile Animal Shelter
7665 Howells Ferry Road
Mobile, AL 36618
(251)574-3647
www.mobilecountyanimals.com

California
The Brittany Foundation
P.O. Box 738
Acton, CA 93510-0738
www.brittanyfoundationonline.org
info@brittanyfoundationonline.org

Change of Heart Pit Bull Rescue
Norco, CA
www.cohpitbullrescue.com

Downtown Dog Rescue
Los Angeles, CA
www.downtowndogrescue.org

Fresno Bully Rescue
8547 W. Herndon Avenue
Fresno, CA 93723
(559) 803-5214
www.fresnobullyrescue.org

It's The Pits
San Diego, CA
(858) 484-0985
www.itsthepits.org

Indiana
Casa Del Toro Pit Bull Education & Rescue
Indianapolis, IN
(317) 956-3398
www.casadeltoro.org

Indianapolis Humane Society
7929 Michigan Road
Indianapolis, IN 46268
(317) 872.5650
www.indyhumane.org

Indy Pit Crew
4170 N. Pennsylvania St.
Indianapolis, IN 46205
(317) 592-9614
www.indypitcrew.org
info@indypitcrew.org

Illinois
Don't Bully My Breed
www.dontbullymybreed.org
dontbullymybreed@aol.com

Louisiana
Animal Rescue New Orleans
271 Plauche St.
New Orleans, LA 70123
(504) 571-1900
www.animalrescueneworleans.org
Arnoinfo@cox.net
(ARNO is struggling with increased intakes and decreased donations in the wake of the Gulf Oil crisis and can really use support).

The Sula Foundation
PO Box 3780
New Orleans, LA 70117
www.sulafoundation.org
info@sulafoundation.org

If you suspect dog fighting in the New Orleans area, call Crimestoppers Hotline at (504) 822-1111 or the S.P.C.A. at (504) 944-7445.

New York
Mayor's Alliance for NYC's Animals
244 Fifth Avenue, Suite R290
New York, NY 10001-7604
(212) 252-2350
www.animalalliancenyc.org

Animal Farm Foundation
PO Box 624
Bangall, NY 12506
(518) 398-0017
www.animalfarmfoundation.org

Animal Haven
251 Centre Street
New York, NY 10013
(212) 274.8511
www.animalhavenshelter.org

Pennsylvania
Hello Bully
4885-A McKnight Road #197
Pittsburgh, PA 15237
412-235-1997
www.hellobully.com
info@hellobully.com

Western Pennsylvania Humane Society
1101 Western Avenue
Pittsburgh PA 15233
(412) 321-4625
www.wpahumane.com

If you suspect dog fighting in the area, call the Pennsylvania SPCA Dog Fighting Hotline at (866) 601-SPCA.

Texas
Heaven Sent Pit Bull Rescue

P.O. Box 1424
Pinehurst, TX 77362
www.heavensentpitbullrescue.com

Operation Kindness
3201 Earhart Dr
Carrollton, TX 75006
(972) 418-7297
www.operationkindness.org

Product Bull Inc. Rescue
203 El Verde Lane
Brownsville, TX 78520
(956) 408-0307
www.productbull.com
mmv@productbull.com

Utah
Best Friends Animal Society
5001 Angel Canyon Road
Kanab, UT 84741-5000
(435) 644-2001
www.bestfriends.org
info@bestfriends.org

Vermont
Good Karma Rescue
Montpelier, VT 05602
www.GoodKarmaRescue.org
GoodKarmaRescue@gmail.com

Travel Resources

To find a comprehensive listing of dog-friendly lodging, restaurants, parks, campgrounds, attractions and more by city, visit www.dogfriendly.com.

For info on great, off-the-beaten-path places to eat, visit www.roadfood.com or buy the book *Roadfood* by Jane and Michael Stern.

Loren and I stayed at the following pet-friendly hotel chains:

La Quinta Inns
(800) SLEEP-LQ
www.lq.com

Motel 6
(800) 4MOTEL6
www.motel6.com

Red Roof Inn
(800) 733-7663
www.redroof.com

Super 8
(800) 800-8000
www.super8.com

"Saving one dog may not change the world, but it means the world to that one dog." - Anonymous

$1 from each copy of "Pit Stops" will benefit The Brittany Foundation